The
Anti-War

Peace Finds the Purpose of a
Peculiar People

Douglas Gwyn

Inner Light Books
San Francisco, California
2016

The Anti-War

This side

Peace Finds the Purpose of a Peculiar People

Other side

Militant Peacemaking in the Manner of Friends

© 2016 Douglas Gwyn
All rights reserved. Except for brief quotations, no part of this publication may be reproduced, stored in a retrieval system, or transmitted, in any form or by any means, electronic, mechanical, photocopy, recorded, or otherwise, without prior written permission.

Editorial and book design: Charles Martin
Copyediting: Kathy McKay
Layout and design: Matt Kelsey

Published by Inner Light Books
San Francisco, California
www.innerlightbooks.com
editor@innerlightbooks.com

Library of Congress Control Number: 2016947701

ISBN 978-0-9970604-3-0 (hardcover)
ISBN 978-0-9970604-4-7 (paperback)
ISBN 978-0-9970604-5-4 (eBook)

The Anti-War

Contents

This Side:

Introduction and Personal Testimony	1
Endnotes	15
Peace Finds the Purpose of a Peculiar People	17
Part 1: A Letter to "Aliens and Exiles"	20
Part 2: The Early Quaker Movement	41
Part 3: Peace Still Finds the Purpose	
of a Peculiar People Today	68
Endnotes	83
Works Cited for the Entire Book	88

Other Side:

Militant Peacemaking in the Manner of Friends	1
Introduction	1
Part 1: A Letter to Martyrs	4
Part 2: Early Quaker Lamb's War	23
Part 3: Capitalism, Empire, and	
the Military-Industrial Complex	41
Part 4: The Anti-War	66
Conclusion: The One, the Alpha	
and the Omega, the X-Covenant	93
Endnotes	95

Introduction and Personal Testimony

This little book will probably confuse and disorient the reader at first glance. Its two main essays are physically and theologically posed in inverse relation to each other. They bore into the issues of war and peace from different vantage points. This arrangement is not an attempt at novelty. It maps my own experience of trying to write about the Quaker peace testimony in the twenty-first century. I didn't plan this structure; I groped my way into it.

The process began with a course I taught with Ben Pink Dandelion at the Woodbrooke Quaker Study Centre in November 2010: The Quaker Peace Testimony: A Tragedy in Three Acts. Building on an earlier collaboration,[1] we presented the early Quaker Lamb's War and its peace testimony as a tragic spirituality. That is, early Friends made a resolute stand for nonviolent witness and were willing to suffer for it. They expected the world's hostility and continuing violence, knowing that the nations had not come to the same surrender to the will of God that they had reached. Their conformity to the cross of Christ was perhaps most succinctly articulated in the actions and writings of James Nayler, most of all in his 1657–58 tract, *The Lamb's War*.

We then proceeded to sketch a history of the Quaker peace testimony, following its various shifts. These generated from shifts in Quaker theology and self-understanding, culminating with the flowering of "Quakerism" and "pacifism" in the twentieth century. We concluded that what modern Friends understand as pacifism is a more ideological, ethically idealistic, and triumphalist formation, in sharp contrast to the tragic sense with which early Friends enacted their peace testimony. That is to say, the existential conviction of early Friends, grounded in their harrowing experience of inward transformation and social stigmatization, has become a more comfortable philosophical position, largely middle-class in social situation, suggesting that peace is ethically better than violence for anyone cool-headed enough to think about it and that peaceful solutions to conflict will triumph wherever reason and enlightened self-interest prevail.

But by the end of the twentieth century, the confidence of modern pacifists had been badly shaken. Lacking the tragic sense of the cross and the human condition, the triumphalist vision of pacifists was chastised by the ravages of Western capitalism and the vast military establishment required to enforce its regime around the world. The overwhelming and unaccountable powers of the present regime drive many to disengagement, others to cynicism, others to spasmodic protests against each new war, and still others to second thoughts about the underpinnings of pacifism. Since Friends tend to look to the vision and example of our founding generation for guidance or justification, it is revealing that in recent decades several writers have cast doubts or pointed up ambiguities regarding the "pacifism" of early Friends. Most recent at the time of this writing is David Boulton's presidential address to the Friends Historical Society meeting in 2013. Drawing on various examples of early Quakers in the army and militias during the 1650s, Boulton's conclusion is: "Whatever this was, it wasn't pacifism."[2] Rosemary Moore also points up the evident inconsistencies in the pacifism of early Friends. But she concludes, with more nuance, that they were not "pacifist in the modern sense."[3]

Meanwhile, three months after the Woodbrooke course, I participated in a conference at Guilford College organized by Chuck Fager in January 2011 marking the fiftieth anniversary of Eisenhower's landmark speech regarding the military-industrial complex. The conference not only recalled Eisenhower's warnings to the American public as he left office; several presentations also showed just how far the military-industrial complex has progressed since then. My presentation charted the social and spiritual formation of the military-industrial complex in light of the Book of Revelation. It came at the end and landed with a resounding thud after so many contemporary and journalistic presentations.

But I felt I was onto something. I had learned much from the way early Friends used Revelation, which was not to predict the future, as most Christian fundamentalists do, but to unveil the larger meaning of their unfolding conflict with the established church in England. Their example provided a bridge between the ancient apocalyptic visions of John and the apocalyptic implications of today's techno-militarism. The chart presented in the essay on the other side of this book expands on the paper I presented at that conference. The chart also influenced the structure of the essay that follows this introduction and ties the book together as a whole.

The essay that follows this introduction treats some of the non-pacifist traits of early Friends that David Boulton presents, but the essay's overall aim is to show the coherent theological framework of the early Christian witness that early Friends reclaimed in their own historical circumstances. Both early Christians and early Friends embodied covenant peoplehood as a divine peacemaking initiative in society. The essay analyzes the inner dynamic of that peoplehood. The essay at the other end of this book analyzes the outward dynamic of early Christians and early Friends in conflict with the violent regimes of their times. Both essays draw conclusions that reframe "pacifism" today—if indeed "pacifism" is a useful word for describing a living faith rather than a fading ideology. The overall title of this book, *The Anti-War*, suggests that a prophetic Christian and Quaker faith is not just opposed to war (i.e., "anti-war" used as an adjective) but is an active *inversion* of war and the unjust social norms that war perpetuates. To state the meaning of "the anti-war" (used as a noun) in positive terms, it is a life of covenant faithfulness with

God, our fellow humans, and the rest of creation. It is, as George Fox put it, "that life and power that takes away the occasion of all wars."

The two essays mirror each other in their sequence from early Christian to early Quaker to present-day dynamics of peacemaking. Hopefully, the four-cornered charting of those dynamics help elucidate the content. The inverted relation between the two essays suggests their different inside-out versus outside-in perspectives. My hope is that this structure not only presents the content helpfully but will also generate further reflection for the reader, as it has for me. Perhaps no more needs to be said here to introduce the book.

But the purpose of this introductory essay is also to speak from my own experience of peacemaking. What can I say that "I know experimentally," to borrow George Fox's classic phrase? I am not much of a peace activist, though I admire those who are. I've written a few letters, signed some petitions, and participated in some vigils, marches, and rallies. I registered as a conscientious objector during the Vietnam War (though the draft ended before I finished school). I've been a war tax resister most of my wage-earning years and even spent a night in jail in 1985 for a nonviolent protest against the U.S. war in Central America. But I don't consider myself an activist.

Since my calling to be a minister in 1968 at age nineteen,[4] my work among Friends has been a long series of sojourns in various sectors of the Religious Society of Friends in the United States and Britain. I have served as a Friends pastor in Indiana, California, and Maine. Interspersed with pastorates, I have also taught on Quaker and biblical subjects at the Pendle Hill and Woodbrooke Quaker study centers. Along the way, I have researched and written on Quaker theology in history. This itinerant pattern emerged early in my ministry.

Introduction and Personal Testimony

While I was in seminary and graduate school in the 1970s, I worked part-time for the American Friends Service Committee (AFSC) in New York on issues of world hunger and international development. I found the systemic (economic and political) issues of justice, peace, and the environment more compelling than the event-driven, reactive politics of the peace movement during the Vietnam War. While with AFSC, Richard Barnet's and Ronald Muller's work in *Global Reach: The Power of the Multinational Corporations*[5] was a revelation for me. I attended a lecture by Seymour Melman on the social costs of the permanent war economy.[6] His analysis was powerful, and I was intrigued by his fiery responses to the neoconservatives who showed up to oppose him. Meanwhile, I was starting to study George Fox. I found Marxist historian Christopher Hill's larger socioeconomic framing of radical religion a vital complement to early Quaker theology.[7]

My theological studies at Union Theological Seminary in New York introduced me to scholarship on the apocalyptic theology of the late Hebrew prophets, the letters of Paul, and the Book of Revelation. Since I had received my call in the apocalyptic year of 1968, this theology had personal resonance for me and interacted helpfully with Marxist theories of revolution. In particular, I was fortunate to take a course on the Book of Revelation with Elisabeth Schüssler Fiorenza in 1975, my last year at Union. Her ongoing work informs this book.

At the same time, I was also participating for the first time in unprogrammed Friends meetings around New York. I had grown up in the liberal Christian wing of the pastoral Quaker stream in Indiana, which still felt like a home to me. But the more universalist and socially progressive ethos of unprogrammed Quaker meetings engaged me in new ways. Most Friends are at home in one stream or the other and quite sure that "their" Friends are the "real Christians" or the "real Quakers."

But I found myself unable to deny the validity of one for the strengths of the other. Both are seriously flawed; both retain a degree of integrity. By the time I finished my PhD in 1982, I believed that the prophetic Christian witness of early Friends offered an evocative example to inspire renewal among Friends across the spectrum (as these essays aim to demonstrate).

These key orienting/disorienting experiences during the 1970s set my course of itinerancy in ministry and established my intellectual affinities. Over the years that have followed, I have reflected theologically on my experiences among the branches of Friends in various lectures and publications.

In *Unmasking the Idols: A Journey among Friends* (1988), I suggested that there is no future for either pastoral or unprogrammed Friends if they continue to emulate either the wider evangelical churches or the wider secular-humanist culture. The riches of our own Quaker tradition offer powerful inspiration for renewal. The point of learning from earlier generations of Friends is not to *conform* to their example but to let it interact with the Spirit's leadings today. The results will *confirm* the strengths of Quaker faith and practice in new ways.

In a Johnson Lecture to the 1990 Friends United Meeting (FUM) triennial, I explored the conversation between Jesus and the Samaritan woman in the Gospel of John to suggest the possibility of covenant renewal between pastoral and unprogrammed Friends. Interestingly, some found the Bible study part of the lecture edifying but felt that my personal story in relation to it was distracting. Others found the Bible study uninteresting but were engaged by my personal story. In any case, little did I know that some in FUM were already strategizing a plan to segregate the two streams once and for all. By the next year, the "realignment" controversy had relegated to obscurity my call to reconciliation. But, the Word is to be preached in season and out of season.

At the 1992 Western Gathering of Friends, I suggested that "realignment" and other manifestations of alienation and conflict among Friends are a Quaker iteration of the "culture wars" that pervade all religious groups in America and the culture at large, with enervating effects on religious groups and their energies for social renewal. Friends manifest the culture wars acutely because Quakers arose at the cusp of transition between the end of the Protestant Reformation and the beginnings of the liberal Enlightenment. Quaker faith and practice at its heart is neither Protestant nor liberal-humanist, but it has been drawn in both directions by these two main poles of Anglo-American history and culture. Again, a deeper listening to the voices of early and traditional Friends can help draw our different branches back to the vine and our common rootstock. I didn't argue for a reunification of Friends but for the possibility that our different branches, through reconciling conversation with one another, can enter into more creative dialogue and perhaps even serve as "olive branches" of peacemaking to the wider culture, where ideological warfare sometimes spills over into outright physical violence.

In a plenary address to the Friends General Conference Gathering of 1997, I addressed the perennial seeking ethos of liberal Quakerism. Drawing on my research into Quaker beginnings, I suggested that the Quaker movement formed out of a convergence between two types of "Seekers." Some were basically Protestants whose search for "primitive Christianity revived" had taken them to radical conclusions. Others were proto-liberals expecting the dawn of a new, progressive age of the Spirit. Early Quaker preaching confirmed and disconfirmed the expectations of both groups by drawing their backward- and forward-looking aspirations into a powerful, unfolding present as they learned to *stand still* in the light of Christ's direct teaching in the conscience. Again, I encouraged contemporary Friends to learn from the faith and practice that so powerfully transformed and motivated early Friends and let the Spirit renew us.[8]

At a 1996 consultation at Pendle Hill, I reflected on my own experience of feeling drawn to both pastoral and unprogrammed, both Christian and universalist Friends. I named this experience "bispiritual": I find vitality and covenantal faithfulness, though differently expressed, among both streams of Friends and resist the binary thinking that judges one correct and the other false. I reflected on the Jerusalem Council in the first decades of the Church, which confirmed both the Jewish identity and the universal extent of the Christian movement. It was a volatile, unstable formula that didn't last very long, but it generated enormous, world-historical energies. Later claims by the Gentile Church that it had superseded Judaism were a triumphalist fabrication that contributed to anti-Semitism over time. I warned liberal Friends that Enlightenment, progressivist claims to supersede Christianity amount to the same triumphalism and that it will prove equally hollow and pernicious over time. By contrast, a truly bipolar faith is both disturbing and energizing.

In a plenary address to the 2005 FUM triennial, I unexpectedly found myself addressing FUM's controversial policy not to hire persons sexually active outside of marriage, particularly homosexuals. I suggested that an overt Christian acceptance of homosexuals and homosexual behavior is not necessarily the "progressive" change that liberal advocates urge. It can just as easily be seen as a forthright witness to the reality that homosexuals have covertly been part of the Church and among its most gifted leaders for 2,000 years. Therefore, to change FUM's staffing policy would not be "moving forward" into a progressively brighter future (the familiar liberal ideology that often strikes conservatives as glib). Rather, the change would amount to "standing fast" more resolutely and openly in the truth of who we are in Christ. I was criticized by some for going "off-message" and disturbing the uneasy peace among FUM's restive constituencies. But others were glad to hear a Friends pastor speak out in this way.[9]

These occasional talks gave me the opportunity to distill the experience of my crisscross movements and years of listening among Friends. My ministry has been *peacemaking,* not as averting violent conflict but as an effort to renew covenantal faith and reconciliation among Friends. As I note elsewhere in this book, the Hebrew word for covenant derives from a verb meaning "to bind," but the Hebrew verb often used to describe making a covenant means "to cut." Covenant renewal is thus both binding and cutting. It strengthens the true basis of our unity *and* renounces the extrinsic elements that keep us apart.

Another image I've more recently found useful in understanding covenantal dynamics is *trimming.* Political theorist Jane Calvert utilizes this sailing term to describe the political logic of William Penn and Quaker constitutional politics in colonial Pennsylvania (I devote some attention to Calvert's work in the essay that follows this introduction). Calvert appears to be uninformed of the more revolutionary covenantal politics of the first Quaker generation and how that politics informed subsequent Quaker constitutional theory in America. But her thesis is compelling in its own right. Quaker politics in Pennsylvania were paradoxical. Anti-Quaker critics complained that Friends were utterly pragmatic in their political maneuvering as they adopted apparently contradictory policies from one moment to the next. But Friends frequently shifted positions with a consistent aim: to remain faithful to the *constitution*, which they understood to be not just a written document but a living, evolving consent among the people. (This political philosophy derived from the early Quaker understanding of covenant as the light abiding in all consciences. Light is received by way of individual consciences, but its purpose is to gather a people that learns in evolving ways to live faithfully to God and with one another. Covenant is an idiom for faithful relationship.)

Calvert utilizes the sailing practice of trimming as a metaphor for this political principle. Shifts of ballast or of the crew's weight from side to side may seem contradictory within the confines of the boat. But these shifts serve to keep the boat on a steady course in relation to a transcendent horizon. The trimmer "remains independently in the middle with a view to the object beyond himself."[10] Both inside and outside government, Quakers engaged in this practice of trimming as the interaction between two core principles: *unity* and *dissent*. Friends consistently sought the unity and health of the colonial polity. But sometimes that unity was best served by their stubborn dissent from unjust and divisive initiatives that arose from other elements within the colony. Calvert suggests that Quaker trimming laid a foundation for the tradition of nonviolent dissent and action in America.

Calvert's work has helped me better understand my own life in ministry. In the apparently contradictory affinities of my Quaker "bispirituality," I have repeatedly divested myself of my lifework on one side of the Quaker divide in order to re-invest it on the other. This pattern has emerged through a search for Quaker *unity* that is also a *dissent* from the elements of current faith and practice that seem to me extrinsic to our tradition and that perpetuate our mutual estrangement. I have made each zig-zag move in relation to the transcendent horizon of God's initial calling and through God's continued leadings, received through sustained spiritual practice.

These repeated self-disenfranchisements have been costly in terms of financial security and some personal relationships. Some Friends find me inconsistent and

Introduction and Personal Testimony

untrustworthy because of my shifting affinities. It has been a *kenosis*, the self-emptying vocation modeled by Christ and emulated by Paul in his itinerant ministry (see Philippians 2:5–8). I find that it manifests the interaction of all three Greek terms for love found in the New Testament. There is *agape*, the sacrificial love that prefers the good of the other over oneself. But *agape* exists in intimate relationship with *eros*, a personal interest in and desire for the other. One cannot prefer the good of the other without some kind of drawing toward the other. In my experience, there has always been an element of attraction in my movement toward the next group of Friends that I would like to know and collaborate with. But my movement in that direction always entails an overturning of what I was doing before, a painful and disorienting transition, and new, unanticipated challenges. In each new phase, however, the interaction of *eros* and *agape* matures into the growth of *philos*: friendship, mutual love, collaborative action, and fruitful outcomes.

I have thus experienced a repeating pattern of self-forgetfulness and emptying, which moves toward self-re-membering and fulfillment, through conversation and collaboration with others and through an ongoing prayerful communion with my Lord. "Lord" is not just traditional language for me. This is the person to whom I appeal, whom I seek to serve, the person who has loved and provided for me through many changes, even if I don't understand very much about this person.

I will not deny that there have also been neurotic aspects to my continuing movement: restlessness with regard to organizational inertia, fear of stagnation, the idealization of someplace else. I have also made some mistakes that I have deeply regretted along the way. A life of errantry, travel without an established path, is prone to error. But I also believe that God has been willing to work my human weaknesses toward divine purposes: i.e., the transcendent horizon that I only half-discern along the way. The wandering life of Abraham,

God's first great covenant partner, has been a model for me over the years.

What I am describing is not heroic. (Abraham is probably best described as an anti-hero. Faith is a minefield of ironies; one is never certain of God's real purposes or one's own faithfulness.) And I've seen little effect from my efforts. But this is the work I have been given, and I have tried to remain faithful in it. So, this is what I know "experimentally" about peacemaking. My experience underlies the two main essays of this book. Others who have been more on the front lines of conflict and war could write other things. But again, this is a time for Friends to take their bearings anew with the peace testimony, to explore the meaning of anti-war as a noun and not only as an adjective. An adjective modifies a noun; it qualifies something that is. But *what are we* as Friends today? Both "Quakerism" and "pacifism" are ideological positions and philosophical affinities that have largely lost their grounding in personal conviction, in a radical way of being in the world. A renewal of militant Quaker faith and practice will be some form of covenant renewal, whatever language Friends choose to ascribe to it. Whatever powerful bonds of shared witness and service it forms among us, whatever things we are led to renounce and denounce, it will be a renewal of "that life and power that takes away the occasion of all wars."

My peacemaking ministry has been grounded in a personal experience of peace. I don't consider myself a mystic, but a prophet. Again, I do not use prophet in any heroic sense but rather as one whose spiritual devotion receives a divine word within. Sometimes that word is something I'm led to speak, or write, or enact to others. Like Isaiah (8:14), I experience that divine word as a sanctuary of peace. Speaking my peace may lead others to the same peace, or they may stumble and be offended by it. I am not in charge of the outcomes but can only be faithful to what I have been given. Part of the purpose of this book is to explore how early Christians and early

Friends generated so much conflict while acting in a spirit of peace. *Prophetic* describes this spirituality more adequately than *mystical*. Mysticism describes an experience of unity with God and all things. Early Christians and early Friends can indeed be described as mystics. But prophecy is the experience of being called to action, given a word from the Lord to speak. Given this difference, Quaker spirituality at its most robust clearly manifests the prophetic.[11]

I also find that when I remain close to the sanctuary of God's Word within, I encounter something of God in other persons. There is something of God's person that dignifies each person, even if they are in rebellion from it. But further, something of God in me will not *allow* me to resort to violence against another person. That doesn't mean that I could never commit violence, but it would be a breach of God's will in my life. So, I pray not to be put to the test. But if I fail the test and resort to violence, I don't have to justify it. I can ask the forgiveness of God and anyone I have hurt. It may also be possible for me to atone for my action with some form of restorative justice. The ideology of pacifism often lacks the acknowledgment that we may fail. The faith that undergirds the peace testimony knows better.

Peacemaking can't always make things come out right. History will continue as tragedy and travesty much of the time. Our role is to be faithful where we are, to advocate peaceful resolutions to conflict, and at times to stand in the way of violent action. But most of all, as a peculiar people with a unique vocation in the world, our calling is to keep renewing and extending the covenantal life that "takes away the occasion of all wars." Through this faithful practice, God will put our witness to larger purposes in the world, purposes beyond our reckoning.

Finally, this book serves as a companion piece to my 2014 book *A Sustainable Life: Quaker Faith and Practice in the Renewal of Creation*, which reframes traditional categories of our faith and practice within the horizon of work for a sustainable world, the overarching challenge of our age. Rather than making sustainability one more thing Friends are concerned about, the book shows how all our practices, from personal spiritual formation through worship and ministry, spiritual discernment, and all our traditional testimonies are about a healthy, balanced way of life on earth. Quaker life is a particular "species" of spiritual and material practice that can work in symbiotic relationship with other such species to rebalance human society and human life on this planet. But again, as affirmed in the preceding paragraph regarding peace, such human purposes will be put to larger purposes beyond our reckoning.

Introduction and Personal Testimony

NOTES

[1] Pink Dandelion, Douglas Gwyn, Rachel Muers, Brian Phillips, and Richard E. Sturm, *Towards Tragedy/Reclaiming Hope: Literature, Theology and Sociology in Conversation* (Aldershot, Hampshire, England: Ashgate, 2004).

[2] David Boulton, "'Elves, Goblins, Fairies, Quakers, and New Lights': Friends in the English Republic," *Journal of the Friends Historical Society* 63 (2012): 3–19. For a different view, see Stuart Masters's review of Gerard Guiton's *The Early Quakers and the 'Kingdom of God': Peace, Testimony and Revolution* (San Francisco: Inner Light Books, 2012) in *Journal of the Friends Historical Society* 64 (2013): 22–25. My own work here shares Masters's understanding of the issues.

[3] Rosemary Moore, *The Light in Their Consciences: The Early Quakers in Britain, 1646–1666* (University Park: Pennsylvania State University Press, 2000), 124.

[4] I describe my calling experience in "The Covenant of Light," in Douglas Gwyn, *Words in Time: Essays and Addresses* (Bellefont, PA: Kimo, 1997), http://quakertheology.org/GwynBook--RV-12-2015.pdf.

[5] Richard J. Barnet and Ronald E. Muller, *Global Reach: The Power of the Multinational Corporations* (New York: Simon & Schuster, 1974).

[6] See Melman's classic work, *The Permanent War Economy: American Capitalism in Decline* (New York: Simon & Schuster, 1976).

[7] See Hill's highly praised *The World Turned Upside Down: Radical Ideas during the English Revolution* (New York: Penguin, 1975).

[8] All three of these addresses can be found in Gwyn, *Words in Time.*

[9] These last two pieces are collected in Douglas Gwyn, *Report from the Middle: Reflections on Divisions among Friends Today* (Boston: Beacon Hill Friends House, 2005).

[10] Jane E. Calvert, *Quaker Constitutionalism and the Political Thought of John Dickinson* (Cambridge: Cambridge University Press, 2008), 13.

[11] I differ with Rufus Jones's mystical interpretation of Quaker spirituality. See Douglas Gwyn, *A Sustainable Life: Quaker Faith and Practice in the Renewal of Creation* (Philadelphia: Quaker Press, 2014), p. 22.

Peace Finds the Purpose of a Peculiar People

As the twenty-first century unfolds, the human condition is in a darkening phase. Islamic revolution continues to spread in the Middle East and Africa, fueled by resentment of the West and a vicious violence more indicative of degenerative patriarchy than the true faith of Islam. The U.S. war on drugs has imprisoned millions at home and created spectral violence among drug cartels in Latin America, eroding civil society and driving thousands to flee and seek asylum in the United States. Democratic governments and institutions around the world have been gutted by kleptocrats, oligarchs, and military-industrial elites. World summits on climate change produce the parlor rhetoric of fine words unmatched by substantive action. Wars are increasingly generated out of struggles over scarce resources. Population growth continues to be the great unmentionable factor in environmental crises of every kind. Various forms of slavery oppress unknown numbers around the world, with women and girls the most exploited. Senseless mass shootings occur regularly, committed by American males who are only the most extreme expression of masculinity in crisis.

Any of us could add to this short but disturbing list. My point is that Friends today live in a world different from the one that gave rise to liberal Quakerism a century ago, before World War I, the first of the twentieth century's great violent convulsions. Liberal renewal generated the most creative and ambitious project of peacemaking in Quaker history and has exerted a wide influence on peacemaking individuals and organizations around the world. But the religious inspiration and personal commitment that fueled liberal Quakerism's most energetic phases have dissipated. Quaker religious convictions have become diffuse, and one hears the commitment to peace fraught with ambivalence in many Friends meetings today. A recent survey among British Friends by Pink Dandelion and research associates finds both of these tendencies growing and converging.[1] Similar trends are evident among North American Friends.

This essay proposes that a tougher-minded and more spiritually resilient witness is required if Friends are to meet the challenges of this century. Commitment will only continue to weaken until we dig down and rediscover the first principles of Quaker faith and purpose in the world. This undertaking requires not only personal soul-searching but deep listening to the prophetic vision of early Friends and the biblical texts that framed it. The present essay is motivated both by a growing concern for the prospects of peace today and by the increasingly fragmented state of the Religious Society of Friends. That fragmentation is evidenced not simply by our long-standing divisions but also by the lack of coherence and purpose within the existing branches. This essay is also motivated by years of study of both Scripture and the witness of early Friends. These sources have nourished my faith and given me hope, even if I cannot be optimistic about our present condition.

This essay posits that *peace finds the purpose of a peculiar people.* The four terms of that simple phrase establish the coordinates of a living Quaker faith. But the biblical framing of these terms, which were so resonant for early and traditional Friends, requires some unpacking for us today. A text from the New Testament, 1 Peter 2:4–17, establishes the coordinates. What follows as Part 1 is a brief commentary on that passage and how it may have described the experience of early Christians. Part 2 then explores the way these same four coordinates defined the early Quaker movement and its peace testimony. I conclude in Part 3 by offering further reflections for our times.

Part 1

A Letter to "Aliens and Exiles"

The First Letter of Peter was probably not written by the fisherman from Capernaum who put down his nets to follow Jesus and later became the central figure in the first years of the Christian movement. Simon Peter was probably martyred in Rome in the mid-60s of the first century, possibly as a victim of Emperor Nero's tactic to scapegoat Christians for the great fire of Rome that occurred in 64. The person writing this letter in Peter's name is neutral toward Rome. The author is not as unconcerned as Paul seems to be in Romans 13, written in the late 50s, but by no means demonizes Rome as John does in Revelation, which was written sometime around the mid-90s. The letter is thought to have been written sometime within the twenty-year span of 73 to 92. It is a general epistle to a variety of congregations proliferating around Asia Minor (modern Turkey; see 1 Peter 1:1) that drew individuals from a range of ethnic and cultural backgrounds.

New Testament interpreter John Elliott analyzes the message of 1 Peter using a social-scientific assessment of its historical context. The letter addresses the conflict early Christians experienced with a conformist society that found them objectionable and worthy of contempt. Ancient and traditional societies were based on codes of honor versus shame, in contrast to the codes of virtue versus guilt familiar to us in modern, industrialized societies. Today, moral assessment tends to be individual and introspective. In the ancient world, it was more group-oriented and confrontational. Honor was closely identified with family, ethnicity, morality, civic duty, and religious piety. Non-conforming individuals and groups were stigmatized, shamed, and marginalized, both socially and economically. In Greco-Roman thought, the ability to feel shame separated humans from the animals. Shamelessness was therefore seen as subhuman, amoral, the realm of deviants and strangers.[2]

Early Christians were shamed, slandered, and marginalized in their neighborhoods for their religious otherness and lack of civic spirit. If Wayne Meeks is correct in his social study of Paul's urban congregations, the gospel may have attracted men and women who had already experienced some kind of social dissonance. Meeks finds among the references to individuals and circumstances in Paul's letters a marked incidence of Jews attracted to Greek culture, Gentiles drawn to Judaism, freed slaves, formerly free individuals fallen into slavery, and women of unusual wealth and independence. The story of a crucified Messiah served as a powerful paradigm for their social experience. Jesus of Nazareth experienced rejection, humiliation, and even death in response to his gospel of forgiveness and reconciliation. Paul's congregations may have been more urban than those addressed by 1 Peter, but it would appear that they faced similar hardships.[3]

According to Elliott, 1 Peter responds to the ostracism faced by early Christians with four key points. First, the true criterion of honor is doing the will of God, not conforming to public opinion. Second, Christ is the paramount example of honor, yet he too was shamed and suffered ultimate rejection. Third, Christians should let their honorable conduct win over hostile neighbors. And fourth, suffering for doing right is itself an honor. Thus, 1 Peter offers an *inversion* of the dominant culture's codes of honor.[4]

These dynamics forged a community with internal cohesion strong enough to face down the malignant attitudes of its neighbors. Its members were slandered as *Christianos*, or "Christian" (4:16), yet for them Christ was the source of grace, not disgrace. They lived like aliens and exiles in their surrounding culture, yet they were at home in the household of God. The household (*oikos*) was the basic building block of Greco-Roman society. It grounded family and ethnic identity, religious devotion, and often economic activity. But households also anchored early Christian communities, which spread in impromptu networks that expanded in unpredictable patterns like the underground rhizomes of an invasive plant. These households drew together motley assortments of people from different ethnic and religious backgrounds, social status, and economic class. As such, they were anathema to the society around them.

These are the general social coordinates of 1 Peter. We may now read the pivotal passage of this unique New Testament letter, 2:4–17 (NRSV)[5]:

> *Come to him, a living stone, though rejected by mortals yet chosen and precious in God's sight, and like living stones, let yourselves be built into a spiritual house, to be a holy priesthood, to offer spiritual sacrifices acceptable to God through Jesus Christ. For it stands in scripture:*
>
> > *"See, I am laying in Zion a stone,*
> >
> > > *a cornerstone chosen and precious;*
> >
> > *and whoever believes in him*
> >
> > > *will not be put to shame."* [Isaiah 28:16]
>
> *To you then who believe, he is precious; but for those who do not believe,*
>
> > *"The stone that the builders rejected*
> >
> > *has become the very head of the corner,"* [Psalm 118:22]
>
> *and*
>
> > *"A stone that makes them stumble,*

> *and a rock that makes them fall."* [Isaiah 8:14]
>
> *They stumble because they disobey the word, as they were destined to do.*
>
> *But you are a chosen race, a royal priesthood, a holy nation, God's own people, in order that you may proclaim the mighty acts of him who called you out of darkness into his marvelous light.*
>
> > *Once you were not a people,*
> >
> > *but now you are God's people;*
> >
> > *once you had not received mercy,*
> >
> > *but now you have received mercy.* [Hosea 1:9, 10]
>
> *Beloved, I urge you as aliens and exiles to abstain from the desires of the flesh that wage war against the soul. Conduct yourselves honorably among the Gentiles, so that, though they malign you as evildoers, they may see your honorable deeds and glorify God on the day of visitation.*
>
> *For the Lord's sake accept the authority of every human institution, whether the emperor as supreme, or of governors, as sent by him to punish those who do wrong and to praise those who do right. For it is God's will that by doing right you should silence the ignorance of the foolish. As servants [or slaves] of God, live as free people, yet do not use your freedom as a pretext for evil. Honor everyone. Love the family of believers. Fear God. Honor the emperor.*

As if to play with Peter's name, the first verses in this passage abound with mentions of stones. And like the stones of a foundation, this passage establishes the movement's orientation toward Christ and (later) toward the Roman Empire. This rich passage deserves a closer, step-by-step examination.

> *Come to him, a living stone, though rejected by mortals yet chosen and precious in God's sight, and like living stones let yourselves be built into a spiritual house, to be a holy priesthood, to offer spiritual sacrifices acceptable to God through Jesus Christ.* (1 Peter 2:4–5)

The "him" referenced here is "the Lord" mentioned at the end of the preceding verse, Jesus the Messiah/Christ. The paradox of a "living stone" sets up the paradoxical identity of Christ and of those who come to him. He was rejected by mortals but chosen and precious in God's sight. And those who come to him become living stones as well, built by the Spirit of Christ into a spiritual house. This is no monolithic institution but one in which the solidity and consistency of the stones is matched by their living, evolving, elastic relationship with one another in Christ. They are not enacting any human plan but rather find themselves being built into a structure whose purpose is beyond their human understanding.

The letter elaborates this "house" (*oikos*) with images and practices from the Hebrew Scriptures and Jewish religion that birthed the movement. This house is "a holy priesthood" offering "spiritual sacrifices." In Hebrew tradition, holiness is the unearthly beauty of the otherworldly God who called Israel to be a people apart. Holiness is a quality apart from the categories and beauties of the rest of creation. It does not imply a negative assessment of the ordinary and earthly, but it does suggest the special calling and set-apart identity of those who are called. Thus, the social otherness they experience as Christians is an outworking of that quality of holiness.

But as this "holy priesthood," the living stones built around Christ are set apart not to enjoy a special status for their own sake; they exist as a sign in service to the wider human society. Their "spiritual sacrifices" mediate *shalom*: that is, they facilitate peaceful relationships with God and in society. That was the role of the Levitical priesthood in ancient Israel, which is the implied model here. These living stones, however, are drawn from many peoples, so this heterogeneous "holy priesthood" offers spiritual sacrifices on behalf of a wider world. So, what are "spiritual sacrifices"? They are "spiritual" in that they arise from the Spirit's leading in particular social contexts, not according to the prescribed rituals of a given religious tradition. They evolve just as the living stones themselves and the house they constitute evolve. The work of peacemaking, of mediating God's *shalom*, is endlessly varied, depending on the conflicts needing to be mediated. They may be psychological, interpersonal, social, cross-cultural, international, material. This work is "sacrificial" in that it offers God's peace to people who may not understand or accept it.

In all this, there is one constant: this house and its peacemaking will be as routinely misunderstood and even hostilely rejected as Jesus was.

> *For it stands in scripture: "See, I am laying in Zion a stone, a cornerstone chosen and precious; and whoever believes in him will not be put to shame"* [Isaiah 28:16]. *To you then who believe, he is precious.* (1 Peter 2:6–7a)

Peter draws here from the prophet Isaiah, who centuries before had envisioned God setting a stone among his people, a cornerstone for the rebuilding of society. God's new social order would be built with "justice the line and righteousness the plummet." This new work would "sweep away the refuge of lies" and annul the "covenant with death" (Isaiah 26:17–18) that had overtaken the harsh, exploitative society Isaiah saw around him.

Whatever Isaiah had seen of this work in his own day, early Christians found it fulfilled in new ways through Jesus and in their own lives as living stones being built around the risen Christ, in the growing networks of peacemaking and mutual aid in the Eastern Mediterranean world. Thus, in spite of all the shaming tactics of their neighbors, they saw something precious developing among them.

> *But for those who do not believe,*
>
> > *"The stone that the builders rejected*
> >
> > *has become the very head of the corner"* [Psalm 118:22],
>
> *and*
>
> > *"A stone that makes them stumble,*
> >
> > *and a rock that makes them fall"* [Isaiah 8:14].
>
> *They stumble because they disobey the word, as they were destined to do."* (1 Peter 2:7b–8)

The Christian community experiences a deep and painful irony. They are being *built* into a spiritual house oriented around Christ, the stone the *builders* reject. Through some mysterious moment of freedom, members of the community have moved away from participating in the usual human culture that builds up through the machinations of emulation, competition and conflict, rewards and rejections. They have begun participating in an organic process that fits them together beyond any human plan. The building culture around them rejected Jesus and continues to reject them because their gospel message and their way of life is not a comprehensible variant of the way the world works. It is so alien that it causes others to stumble. People are scandalized ("a rock that makes them fall" is a translation of *petra skandalou*). The prophet Isaiah had experienced this in his day (the eighth century BCE) when his own people were scandalized by his prophetic call to social justice and peacemaking. Yet for him, the very same prophetic word of the Lord was like a sanctuary (Isaiah 8:14). It both caused him to be rejected and made the rejection bearable.

The community built around Christ is similarly prophetic. Their spiritual house feels like a sanctuary to them but offends others. Peter adds, "They stumble because they disobey the word, as they were destined to do." That sounds like a harsh judgment to us. But it is worth noting that we can see something of its truth around us. The social pressures of our culture exert a powerful conforming influence on us, almost determining our existence. The moments of freedom when that spell is broken and we can make real changes in ourselves and our society come not by our own power. They are our faithful response to a gracious interruption of our lives by a power from beyond us. That power and our response shift the very nature of our being. Our awareness that true freedom is a gift and not a personal accomplishment keeps us humbly open to divine motions in our hearts. It also makes us more gracious, patient, and hopeful toward others. It makes us better peacemakers.

Thus, we become a people created out of nothing by the way we have responded to a *call*. Peter continues:

> *But you are a chosen race, a royal priesthood,*
> *a holy nation, God's own people.* (1 Peter 2:9a)

Instead of "God's own people," the King James Version renders the Greek here as "a peculiar people." This was an important concept for both early Christians and early Friends, but it requires some unpacking for us today.

Peter draws here from the calling of Israel in Hebrew Scripture. In Exodus 19, the Lord tells the Israelites at Sinai,

> *You have seen . . . how I bore you on eagles'*
> *wings and brought you to myself. Now*

> *therefore, if you obey my voice and keep my covenant, you shall be my treasured possession out of all the peoples. Indeed, the whole earth is mine, but you shall be for me a priestly kingdom and a holy nation.* (Exodus 19:4–6)

This language is echoed in Deuteronomy 14:

> *You are children of the Lord your God. You must not lacerate yourselves or shave your forelocks for the dead. For you are a people holy to the Lord your God; it is you the Lord has chosen out of all the peoples on earth to be his people, his treasured possession.* (Deuteronomy 14:1–2)

"Treasured possession" is rendered "peculiar treasure" in the King James translation of 1611. "Peculiar" derives from the Latin *peculium*, meaning personal possession. But, of course, "peculiar" can also mean odd or strange. That's the only meaning still current today.

So the Israelites are not to emulate the cultural practices of their neighbors (obscurely referred to in the passage as laceration and shaving rituals). Instead, they are to live in covenant with God and with one another. Certainly, the whole earth belongs to the Lord, but Israel is a holy nation, a treasured possession of the Lord. Of course, Israel is part of God's creation, the whole earth and its many peoples, and thereby given to the ordinary laws of physics, genetic codes, and human tendencies. But Israel has also been chosen to act out something extra-ordinary. God is working out something peculiar with this people: to demonstrate divine holiness to the peoples of the earth and to be a priestly kingdom that mediates God's *shalom* among the nations. This holiness is profoundly other; it simply does not compute with the laws of nature and the sociology of human interaction. It is God's own nature. It is good, but it is good in ways that don't always fit the categories of human reckoning.

Again, this is the continuing scandal of the stone rejected by the builders and of the living stones that are being built around it. The otherness of this people is defined by the transcendent Other who has called them together. They don't exist as God's "treasured possession" for their own sake but for the sake of communicating God's strange beauty to others. The radical Otherness of God relativizes all kinds of otherness among peoples and in creation, so nothing human or in all creation should be alien to this people. Peacemaking begins here. And this is why God's "peculiar people" have peace finding their purpose. Their very otherness creates new possibilities of relatedness and peace among all peoples.

Indeed, Peter continues, this new people has been called into being

> *in order that you may proclaim the mighty acts of him who called you out of darkness into his marvelous light.*
>
> *Once you were not a people,*
>
> *but now you are God's people;*
>
> *once you had not received mercy,*
>
> *but now you have received mercy.* (1 Peter 2:9b–10)

Like Elijah on Mount Horeb (1 Kings 19:11–13), this people has experienced the "mighty acts" of God not in the special effects of earthquake, wind, or fire but in the hearing of the gospel message and the perception of a still, small voice calling them to a new life. We exist to communicate and extend this liberating call from God. This "marvelous light" makes our former existence look like darkness. It is light precisely because we see ourselves and others in a profoundly new and empathetic way, no longer beholding one another with envy or contempt and no longer aiming to emulate or compete with each other.

The early Church was drawn from a variety of cultures, religions, and ethnic identities. Its members were not "a people." The call of God—and only the call of God—made them a people. Few of them had formerly enjoyed much honor, or "mercy," in their society. But now they have received an astonishing mercy, and they pass it on with the same generosity toward others as they proclaim "the mighty acts of him who called you."

Thus ends the description of the peculiar people, the "treasured possession" of God. They are built around Christ who, in the words of the Letter to the Hebrews, "has taken his seat at the right hand of the throne of God" (12:2). They are with Christ at God's right hand, chosen to be a people for God's specific purposes among the nations. But God is *ambidextrous*. The divine also works in secret, ironic, left-handed ways in the wider world, among people and nations that may not know God or aim to serve God's purposes. People's intentions, good or bad, can be bent toward divine intentions through patterns beyond human comprehension. This paradoxical sense of God's purposes in society and history is crucial to understanding the early Christian and early Quaker commitment to peace. I will say more about it a little later.

Precisely at this juncture, Peter turns to the interaction of the beloved community with the wider world.

> *Beloved, I urge you as aliens and exiles to abstain from the desires of the flesh that wage war against the soul. Conduct yourselves honorably among the Gentiles, so that, though they malign you as evildoers, they may see your honorable deeds and glorify God on the day of visitation.* (1 Peter 2:11–12)

These are individuals who once fit in with prevailing categories and norms, or at least struggled to fit in. Now they are a truly a people living out of place, like aliens and exiles. They once learned from their elders and peers what to desire and what to strive for. Now they live at some remove from those acquired tastes.

"The desires of the flesh" does not mean simply physical drives or sensual yearnings. Rather, the Greek word *sarx*, translated as "flesh" here and in the letters of Paul, generally has more to do with a self-determined existence and ego-driven behavior. The ego generates desires that make war on the soul. The Greek word *psyche* is translated as "soul" here. It is "mind" in the fullest sense, or "personality" in its deepest, abiding registers. Ego-driven desires make conquest of the soul. They turn us into demanding, competing, consuming, and conflicting persons. It is not just a war upon the soul. When the flesh wins that war in us, it moves outward, forming competing classes and power blocs that generate conflicts in society and wars among nations.

Similar teaching comes from the Letter of James:

> *Those conflicts and disputes among you, where do they come from? Do they not come from your cravings that are at war within you? You want something and do not have it; so you commit murder.* (James 4:1–2a)

God's call reorients our minds and shifts the very nature of our being. It also reveals the deepest motives of hatred, conflict, and war. But, it also opens the wellsprings of mercy and compassion.

Therefore, Peter counsels early Christian congregations to conduct themselves honorably in the world, to live as paragons of virtue among their pagan neighbors even though they are indeed "maligned as evildoers." There is outside evidence for this slander by the early second century. For example, the Roman provincial official Tacitus noted that Christians in Asia Minor were "hated because of their vices" and "anti-social tendencies." He offered no details and had no direct knowledge of Christians. Such slanders were common against nonconformists in ancient, shame-based societies. But their night-time dinners ("the Lord's Supper") and their disregard for local civil-religious observances were bound to arouse suspicion. The Roman historian Suetonius described Christians as "animated by a novel and dangerous superstition."[6] Again, no details are given, but there is evidence that early Christian avoidance of meat sacrificed to idols hurt the business of butchers in some towns, contributing to their unpopularity.

But Peter views these problems from an eschatological (end-time) perspective. He believes, like most early Christians, that the crucifixion and resurrection of Jesus have inaugurated a turn of the ages, which will soon reach its climax. A "day of visitation," Christ's manifestation in some form more obvious than his presence by the Spirit, will soon confirm the new reality these Christians are already living. But Peter's point is not about divine retribution for all those who don't "get it" and presently malign Christians. Instead, the "honorable deeds" of Christians will help them see the light at last and "glorify God." Again, peacemaking includes the willingness to suffer rejection and even violence in hope that the consciences of the violent and unjust may yet be reached. No one is beyond God's redemption. At the same time, however, no one in God's right hand is exempt from sharing in the sufferings of Jesus in this drama of redemption.

Meanwhile, Peter offers rather pragmatic counsel, similar to Paul's advice to the churches in Rome in the 50s (see Romans 13):

> *For the Lord's sake accept the authority of every human institution, whether of the emperor as supreme, or of governors, as sent by him to punish those who do wrong and to praise those who do right. For it is God's will that by doing right you should silence the ignorance of the foolish.* (1 Peter 2:13–15)

This advice is not patriotic or even conformist but holds civil power as largely irrelevant to the divine power coursing through these new Christian networks. In other words, get along with the powers as much as possible; they're not where the action is.

"For the Lord's sake accept" ("be subject to" is a better translation of the Greek) the chain of command, from the emperor on down. That is, follow the example of Jesus, who did not resist power or try to seize it but unsettled it from below. As a subject of the Roman Empire, Jesus didn't necessarily obey its commands. At his trial, when Jesus refused to answer Pilate, the governor threatened to crucify him. Jesus responded, "You would have no power over me unless it had been given you from above" (John 19:11). Pilate perhaps understood "from above" as the chain of Roman command that had placed him in power in Judea. But Jesus would have discerned the left hand of God behind Pilate's temporal power. Pilate's threat to crucify Jesus was certainly real, but Jesus' response belittled the provincial governor as a pawn in a game he could not understand.

Peter acknowledges that civil power does at least provide some degree of order and justice, "to punish those who do wrong and to praise those who do right." In so doing, it provides the minimal conditions under which "by doing right you should silence the ignorance of the foolish." Hence, the order maintained by civil society provides the social space within which Christian life may communicate to others and spread.

> *As servants* [or slaves] *of God, live as free people, yet do not use your freedom as a pretext for evil.* (1 Peter 2: 16)

The Christian is accountable to God and thus not free to do everything that is permitted in civil society. Yet that servitude to divine will produces a paradoxical freedom in relation to civil society. These newly created "aliens and exiles" are not bound by the same pressures of conformity, emulation, and competition that drive others. Their freedom is an opportunity to do good, even if that goodness is not always understood or appreciated.

Peter concludes this section of the letter with a concise epigram, the very form of which bolsters its content:

> *Honor everyone. Love the family of believers.*
> *Fear God. Honor the emperor.* (1 Peter 2:17)

The first and last of these imperatives define the Christian relationship to the wider society. Honor everyone, including the emperor. Respect for all persons includes those in power, but it also relativizes them to the whole. Meanwhile, the second and third imperatives define the relationships among the Christian community and to its Lord. Love the family of believers. Fear God. The grace of the beloved community, which knows your true worth, makes bearable the thankless task of honoring everyone, despite their misunderstanding and hostility. Likewise, when you fear God—that is, live in awe of the one who has called you into "this marvelous light" and made you strangely free—you lose your fear/awe of the emperor and can simply honor him as another human being.

In a similar vein, the Letter to the Hebrews remarks, "It is a fearful thing to fall into the hands of the living God" (Hebrews 10:31). It is not that one has fallen into the hands of an ogre. Rather, one lives in the right hand of God, a beloved child of God and a devoted servant of divine purposes. But one also lives in a wider world of conflict and confusion, where the left hand of God works only in more oblique and ironic ways. That is, the Christian has consecrated his or her freedom to God's will but is paradoxically free from the world's expectations (as noted earlier). Others in society have retained their personal freedom but live in fear of the human institutions that the Christian simply honors (if not always conforming to their demands). He or she sees through and past them, searching for evidence of God's left hand working through heedless institutions and apparent happenstance. The Christian may suffer or die from the machinations of confused or malign institutions—but he or she will live in fellowship with the crucified Lord, not in slavish fear.

This providential sense of the two hands of God in personal experience and human history is crucial to understanding the faith and practice of both early Christians and early Quakers. Without it, the nonviolent witness of both movements remains opaque to our modern minds.

To conclude this close reading of 1 Peter 2:4–17, I have charted out the four key terms in this essay's title and the ways they are manifested in the text.

**PEACE FINDS THE PURPOSE
OF A PECULIAR PEOPLE**

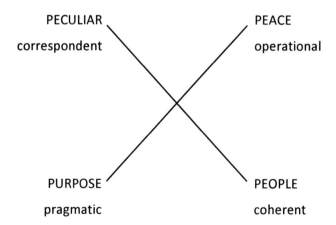

This is a schematic I have developed in earlier books and essays.[7] It is a model for analyzing various truth-claims or meaning systems. It utilizes four standard philosophical accounts of truth and puts them into an interactive framework. Let us examine these four points as they manifest in the early Christian writing of 1 Peter 2:4–17.

People and *Peculiar*. A *people* is a collective with a coherent set of beliefs and practices—coherent at least to them. Others may find their beliefs strange and their practices offensive, as in the case of Roman attitudes toward early Christians. Moreover, that coherence may be difficult for the group to maintain against outside norms and opinions. Inspirational, hortatory communications like 1 Peter were aimed to bolster clarity and courage. The *coherence* theory of truth emphasizes that any particular truth is reckoned within a consistent and harmonious system of truths and values that give it meaning. That system is the frame of reference that gives coherent meaning to any individual point of reference within it. Early Christians derived crucial identity and meaning from their shared faith and practices, both because they were at such variance with prevailing outlooks and because many of them did not enjoy high rank or a coherent status in the wider society (recall Meeks's suggestion that many who joined Paul's congregations had already experienced some kind of social dissonance). And not only the beliefs and ethics but the *people themselves* provided the frame of reference for the participants. As Paul writes to the Church at Corinth, "You are a letter of Christ . . . written not with ink but with the Spirit of the living God, not on tablets of stone but on the tablets of human hearts" (2 Corinthians 3:3). "Reading" one another's integrity and courage helped each person understand the faith and practices better.

At the same time, however, it was not just the oddity of their strange coherence that made them peculiar to others. They were peculiar to God, God's "treasured possession." They were *called* to be this people. The personal experience of calling they shared (no doubt with many variations) provided the point of reference, without which the collective frame of reference would have been arbitrary and meaningless, sheer dogma. This aspect partakes of *correspondence* theory, the most commonsensical account of truth. Bertrand Russell, a leading modern proponent, stated the case succinctly: "Truth consists in some form of correspondence between belief and fact." The beliefs of this peculiar people were established by the facts of each participant's personal experience of God's calling.

So, "peculiar" and "people" are two aspects of early Christian truth that existed in a dynamic, mutually qualifying relationship. There were differences of experience and understanding, to be sure (well attested by Paul's argumentative letters). And both experience and understanding were evolving as the movement matured and continued to interact with its environment. But this basic dynamic between frame of reference and point of reference was constant and necessary. Unlike a static painting, whose framing establishes our point of view, experience and understanding are in constant conversation over time as circumstances change.

Peace and *Purpose*. The second dialectical pairing stands in dialectical relationship to the first pair. The first pair defines the *being* of the peculiar people. This second pair defines their *doing*: that is, the more action-oriented modes of truth, the interaction of means and ends. *Peace* is the *means* peculiar to the people of God. If peace were the end, the goal, they would never attain it. Or, as twentieth-century Quaker activist A. J. Muste put it, "There is no way to peace; peace is the way." In the passage under our consideration, peace comes into the equation of truth as early Christians "abstain from the desires of the flesh that make war upon the soul." This steady practice of non-attachment is "the cross of our Lord Jesus Christ, by which the world has been crucified to me, and I to the world," as Paul vividly testifies in Galatians 6:14. Bearing this cross with patience toward ourselves and others is the way we "work out [our] own salvation with fear and trembling" (Philippians 2:12).

I noted earlier that peace begins as we are liberated one step at a time from the competitive and conflictive machinations of our culture. That way of personal and interpersonal peace moves further out into the world as our "spiritual sacrifices" model and mediate God's *shalom*, an equitable and peaceful life, to the wider social order. This work partakes of the *operational* theory of truth, which asserts that for every proposition there is an appropriate procedure/means of verification. Hence, the Christian believes that Christ is the Prince of Peace (Isaiah 9:6). But that belief must be verified by the Christian's manner of life. In other words, the community's conviction of peace with God (in traditional terms, justification) must be tested through processes of reconciliation with others (sanctification of life).

At the same time, this peacemaking manner of Christian life discovers the *purpose* of the Church in the world. The Church exists to "proclaim the mighty acts of him who called you out of darkness into his marvelous light." Or, as Paul summarizes,

> *All this is from God who reconciled us to himself through Christ, and has given us the ministry of reconciliation; that is, in Christ God was reconciling the world to himself.* (2 Corinthians 5:18–19)

We know that this is our mission, our purpose: to reconcile the peoples of the world to one another and to the oneness of God. But we can only grope forward in it by following the process of peace/reconciliation a step at a time, "for we walk by faith, not by sight" (1 Corinthians 5:7). Here, we come to the *pragmatic* dimension of truth, which defines the end/goal of action, the purpose of a peculiar people. The pragmatic philosophical account of truth, according to William James, suggests that true beliefs are those provoking actions with desirable results. In one sense, the Church exists simply and solely to glorify God, to manifest God's otherworldly holiness, as we heard attested in Exodus and Deuteronomy. But that purpose finds worldly concreteness through the processes of peacemaking/reconciliation in the world.

The interaction of ends and means is as fluid as the interaction of frame and point of reference. Once the Church began to be harnessed to the purposes of the Roman Empire in the fourth century, it was unmoored from God's purposes in calling them to be a people. Peace and reconciliation continued in a variety of ways, to be sure, but the Church lost its larger sense of purpose and fell prone to the temptations of power, which in turn led to religious repression and the sanctification of state violence. Meanwhile, through the imperial-sponsored church councils, doctrinal coherence eclipsed the sense of conviction that had come with the distinct sense of God's call. It was no longer God calling to liberation and reconciliation; it was the Church calling for civil coercion.

Perhaps it is not surprising that, once the Radical Reformation of Anabaptists on the Continent and Quakers in Britain broke the spell of the state over the Church, a more thoroughgoing and programmatic commitment to peace re-emerged, together with an intensified emphasis upon personal experience. These radical reformers denounced the state-sponsored churches as living in "apostasy," a turning away from God's purposes.

With that observation, let us now shift our attention toward the Quaker renewal of the early Christian dynamic just analyzed. "Quaker" was an epithet applied by hostile critics and persecutors (similar to "Christian" in 1 Peter 4:16), but "Children of the Light" and "Friends of the Truth" or "Friends in the Truth" were the names early Friends preferred for themselves. The dynamics of faithfulness to truth were manifested in a fresh way in the first, revolutionary phase of Quaker faith and practice in England of the 1650s.

Part 2

The Early Quaker Movement

The background of Quaker beginnings in the closing years of the English Civil War are briefly treated in the essay on the other side of this book. Reading the *Journal* of George Fox, the central figure in the early movement, one can hardly tell there's a war raging around him as he comes of age in the Midlands of England in the 1640s. Like many young, idealistic hyper-Puritans of that time, Fox was caught up in the drama of his own spiritual upheavals and a desperate longing to be part of the true Church. By the latter 1640s, there were thousands of dropouts, dubbed "Seekers," from the existing church options in England. Some roamed mournfully alone like young Fox, while others participated in a variety of experimental groups.[8] As the focus of this essay is on the development of the peace testimony from the internal dynamics of the Quaker movement, I will not go into the spiritual transformation of Fox and his apostolic calling to found a new people of God.[9]

By 1647, George Fox was itinerating around the Midlands, developing a network of quiet worship groups calling themselves the Children of the Light. They gathered, probably in silent worship, to be taught directly by Christ's light within them, without regular leadership. They seem not to have been politically engaged and didn't attract much attention or trouble, though the Presbyterian clergyman Thomas Edwards may have been referring to Fox in his disapproving reference to an unnamed shoemaker spreading heretical doctrines in that region.[10] Fox preached the perfecting moral power of Christ's light/spirit in the human heart/conscience. He was radicalized, however, in

October 1650, when he was arrested for preaching his Christian perfectionism to a group of soldiers in Derby.

Tried for blasphemy, Fox was convicted and imprisoned in Derby for six months. He was near release when the Parliamentary army tried to recruit him to fight against a Royalist uprising. Fox flatly refused:

> I told them I lived in the virtue of that life and power that took away the occasion of all wars, and I knew from whence all wars did rise, from the lust according to James's doctrine [James 4:1–2a, noted earlier in this essay]. . . . I told them I was come into the covenant of peace, which was before wars and strifes were.[11]

Note that Fox was not refusing that particular war (indeed, his political sympathies were strongly with Parliament's cause). His position was against all war. But more fundamentally, it was a disavowal of the spiritual and social mechanisms of greed, envy, and competition that generate "the occasion of all wars." For this stubborn refusal, he was kept in prison at Derby for another six months.

When Fox was finally freed from prison late in 1651, he soon attracted a number of gifted prophets and preachers, men and women who sparked a rapidly expanding grassroots movement, first in the north of England, then quickly spreading to the south and on to Wales, Scotland, and America. The movement aroused much more conflict and persecution than the earlier Children of the Light had in the Midlands. Nicknamed "Quakers" for their trembling in worship, their spiritual formation was a deep immersion in the "inward cross" of Christ, the light in their consciences, which led them to convictions and commitments strongly similar to those of the first Christians. Fox's spiritual counsel in these early years set followers on a powerful spiritual and moral regimen that freed them from the conformist, competitive, and violent tendencies of the culture around them. They were liberated to recognize and follow the unmediated presence and teaching of Christ within. But this strongly countercultural spirituality soon rendered them "aliens and exiles" in the Puritan culture around them.

In his first published tract, *To All That Would Know the Way to the Kingdom* (1653), Fox wrote:

> The first step of peace is to stand still in the light (which discovers things contrary to it) for power and strength to stand against that nature which the light discovers: here grace grows, here is God alone glorified and exalted, and the unknown truth, unknown to the world, made manifest.[12]

Note that peace is the means, from the very first step *of* peace (congruent with Thich Nhat Hanh's axiom, "Peace is every step."). Note also that the end/purpose is the glory of God, whose truth remains unknown to the world.

But this glory has earthly, socioeconomic implications.

> The free grace of God is the saints' teacher, which teacheth them to deny ungodliness and worldly lusts, to live righteously and godly (like God) in this evil present world. . . . Oh how doth all the creation groan under this bondage of corruption! the Lord is pouring out his spirit upon all flesh that his sons and daughters may prophesy up and down this great city, and none shall make them afraid, crying for justice, crying for righteousness, crying for equity.[13]

Note how the truth that emerges among them first teaches them to renounce the immoral, inequitable, and violent norms of society. Then it sends them out to denounce those same norms. Fox alludes here to the irrepressible campaign of preaching and prophecy that the first Friends waged in markets, streets, and parish churches. The "great city" is Babylon, the prototypical culture of corruption (see the essay on the other side of this book).

Fox continues by defining the Church:

> the church in God, is not an imitation, gathered from the letter, nor is a high-flown people in their imaginations, but are they who are born again of the immortal seed, by the word of God . . . which the world knows not. . . . For the church is the pillar and ground of truth, gathered by the eternal power that was before [the] letter was.[14]

The English Reformation had seen the emergence of many chapter-and-verse reconstructions of the New Testament Church. The Civil War decade had also seen the emergence of experimental groups with exalted claims to mystical experience that didn't bear out in their moral lives. In contrast to both, Fox describes a Church gathered in terms similar to the description discussed above in 1 Peter. The people of God gathered around the living Christ has coherence; it is the pillar and ground of truth. It is not gathered by a mechanistic imitation of primitive Christianity but by each participant's corresponding experience of God's call and Christ's new birth within. The power required to wage nonviolent direct action in the world comes from being part of such a reborn and unified people. Individuals acting out of their own strength and imagination cannot sustain it.

Fox makes the peaceful means of the movement still more explicit in a 1652 letter to Friends:

> Friends,—That which is set up by the sword, is held up by the sword; and that which is set up by spiritual weapons, is held up by spiritual weapons, and not by carnal weapons. The peacemaker hath the kingdom, and is in it; and

hath the dominion over the peace-breaker, to calm him in the power of God.

And Friends, let the waves break over your heads. There is rising a new and living way out of the north, which makes the nations like waters. . . . The days of virtue, love, and peace, are come and coming, and the Lamb had and hath the kings of the earth to war withal, and to fight withal, who will overcome with the sword of the spirit, the word of his mouth; for the Lamb shall have the victory.[15]

The movement that early Friends called the "Lamb's War" aimed to rebuild English society from the base, with the Lamb/Christ/light within each conscience as its rightful sovereign authority.[16] This breathtaking, nonviolent, revolutionary program met with increasingly violent resistance, including mob attacks and official repression—hence the advice to "let the waves" of persecution "break over your heads." The language from the Book of Revelation (i.e., its visions of the Lamb and the Word of God in chapters 14 and 19) is typical of Quaker rhetoric of the first decade. Revelation served as a key text for early Friends in demystifying the state-enforced Church and other unjust and repressive social structures, as well as a manifesto for resisting and disempowering them (for more on Revelation and the Lamb's War, see the essay on the other side of this book).

Although the Book of Revelation and early Friends took a more strongly oppositional position toward civil authority than we find in 1 Peter and the letters of Paul, their basic commitment to *be subject* to civil authority and bear its persecution was the same. But early Friends also lived in a nascently democratic society, in contrast to the Roman Empire. So they petitioned Oliver Cromwell and other tolerant leaders in both Parliament and the army for relief from persecution. Indeed, the army more or less ruled the country during much of the chaotic 1650s and tended to tolerate Friends more than Parliament did. Hence, Quaker writings from that decade evince some affinity with the army, but in its role as a juridical person rather than as a military force.

In fact, during the first two years of the movement, some soldiers became Quakers and saw no need to leave the army. But in 1654, when they refused to swear a new oath of loyalty to Oliver Cromwell (early Friends followed the counsel of Jesus in Matthew 5:33–37 against swearing oaths), they were purged from the ranks. Even twenty years later, Fox complained about this in his *Journal*.[17] Early Friends in the army and early Quaker political sympathies with the army have been a point of some confusion to present-day scholars and pacifists. This matter requires some clarification.

The relation of the Quaker movement to civil authority found focus in a 1655 meeting between Fox and Oliver Cromwell, Lord Protector of the Commonwealth. Fox had been arrested, along with other suspicious persons, when news surfaced of a plot to assassinate Cromwell. Fox was given an audience with Cromwell and protested his innocence regarding all such plots. He followed up the conversation with a letter disavowing violence "against thee, Oliver Cromwell, or any man." He described his mission:

> to turn people from the darkness to the light, and to bring them from the occasion of war and from the occasion of the magistrate's sword, which is a terror to the evil doers who act contrarily to the light of the Lord Jesus Christ . . . [which is] a protection to them that do well and not evil. . . . From under the occasion of that sword I do seek to bring people [see Romans 13:1–5]. My weapons are not carnal but spiritual, and "my kingdom is not of this world" [see John 18:36].[18]

Thus, Fox claimed that, as they turned to the light and entered the revolutionary space of the Lamb's War, Friends lived a life that offered no "occasion" to just laws that prohibit injustice and violence. In effect, they lived in a different realm, even if still on English soil. To the extent that Friends had anything to do with civil authority, it owed them its protection as model citizens. By invoking Jesus' words to Pilate in the Gospel of John, Fox testified to the sovereign authority of the realm that Friends occupied.

But because the army was in direct control of the country at that time, Fox inserted a special clause in the same paragraph regarding the role of soldiers: "Such soldiers as are put in that place [i.e., the role of civil power] no false accusers must be, no violence must do, but be content with their wages."[19] Fox here echoes the counsel of John the Baptist to soldiers in Luke 3:14 and puts the apparent contradiction of Quaker soldiers in perspective. Friends might perform a variety of civil services, even in the military, but without violence or abuse of power.

Meanwhile, Fox was not unsympathetic to Cromwell in the daunting task of drawing together a fragmenting nation. In a letter sent ahead of their meeting, Fox had counseled,

> Live in the wisdom of the life of God, that with it thou mayest be ordered to his glory, and order his creatures to his glory. And be still and silent from thy own wisdom, wit, craft, subtilty, or policy that would arise in thee, but stand single to the Lord, without any end to thyself [i.e., self-interest].[20]

Thus, Fox sought to draw civil power and the Quaker movement, the left and right hands of God, closer together.

But over the next year, the initially tolerant Cromwell was alienated by the intolerable assault Quakers continued to spread against the national Church. Widespread disruption of parish services is indicative of the revolutionary, rather than reformist, impetus of the movement in its first decade. Persecutions against Friends were intensified as Cromwell desperately sought a tenable political settlement for the Commonwealth.

Quakers and other radical groups grew discouraged. A group of Fifth Monarchists attempted armed rebellion in 1657. Some in government thought that Quakers were involved. Quaker spokesman Edward Burrough responded:

> The Kingdom of Christ is setting up, and it is not of this world, neither shall be exalted, nor advanced, by worldly policy, and worldly wisdom, nor by carnal weapons. . . . You that are waiting for the Kingdom of Christ . . . seek for it where it may be found . . . through suffering must the Kingdom of Christ be set up.[21]

When Cromwell died in 1658, the Commonwealth slowly unraveled. Fox grieved as he saw by 1659 that "the powers had hardened themselves, persecuting Friends . . . crucifying the Seed, Christ, both in themselves and in others. And at last they fell a-biting and devouring one another until they were consumed one of another."[22]

That year Fox published a tract that shocks modern-day pacifists. In it, Fox denounces the generals for their abandonment of the revolutionary cause and for enriching themselves with their new-found power:

> Oh! How men have fallen from that which they were at first, when thousands of us went in front of you, and were with you in the greatest heat, who looked not for the spoil, but the good of the nations, and now thus should be served by those that are sat down in the possession of

the spoil of our enemies, that they should requite us so in the end![23]

He goes on to suggest that instead of enriching themselves at the expense of defeated Royalists, the army should have taken the revolution on to Spain "and required the blood of the Innocent shed there," to make them "offer up the Inquisition to you," and then on to Rome, to make "the Pope offer up torture-houses and wracks and Inquisition." "This you should have seen done in the power, when you had been the dread of all Nations." Indeed, the crowned heads of Europe had been deeply shaken by the execution of Charles I and the proclamation of an English Commonwealth in 1649. But the imploding politics of the next decade put them at ease. Here Fox affirms the (left) hand of God at work in the Civil War and even proposes that the army's military revolution should have expanded to overthrow the horrors of the Inquisition (see the pre-Quaker writings of Gerrard Winstanley and Joseph Salmon reflecting on the Civil War, discussed in the essay on the other side of this book).

Fox contrasts the regressive and self-serving policies of the army with the renewed fervor and the different revolutionary mode of the Quaker movement:

> Oh! The Lord's truth, the Lord's power, and the Lord's arm is more dear to us than all, who have not sat down in the spoil of our Enemies, who are come to the Lord who hath given us victory, and hath brought us to the light that takes away the occasion and root of the wars.[24]

But instead of recognizing and defending this new revolutionary movement, "You turned against and put them in prison that struck at the root." The nonviolent social revolution of the Lamb's War attacked the *basis* of an unjust society and its repressive religion, not just one version of it (again, see the essay on the other side of this book).

But the left and right hands of God had moved decisively apart. In the same tract, Fox diagnosed the spiritual malaise that had spread over the 1650s:

> Deceit is grown to such height that men have been afraid of one another, to do justice, and own the innocent; but the general universal spirit in mankind hath been imprisoned, that men have not stood everyone on his own legs in the power of God, and so through flattery, and fair speeches, and feigned words, have deceived, and clogged, and brought one another into thralldom . . . the just lies in prison in themselves, and they cause it to be imprisoned in the general, and that is it which will not let loose, nor set free, and it is impossible it should until it be freed within. . . . The power of God must break the prison-doors open within before he set the prison door open without; and that is the Arm, the Hand, the Power (and not with men's words) which we will have unity withal, who are come to the kingdom that stands in power, of which there is no end.[25]

The imprisonment of Friends and other radicals manifested outwardly the imprisonment of the power of God in the hearts of rulers. Only a surrender to that power within could lead to true liberation in society. These are the agonized conclusions of one who had hoped the left and right hands of God might be reconciled. But that relationship, paradoxical at best, had become an outright contradiction.

This last year of the Commonwealth was a chaotic succession of alliances, changes in regime, plots, and uprisings. Given the strong Quaker preference for an English Commonwealth as the optimal political space to allow the continued expansion of the Lamb's War, some Friends joined militias to stave off the growing momentum for a return to monarchy. Fox wrote that summer to warn them against "that snare":

> All Friends, everywhere, keep out of plots and bustling and the arm of the flesh, for all these are amongst Adam's sons in the Fall, where they are destroying men's lives. . . . All that pretend to fight for Christ they are deceived, for his kingdom is not of this world, therefore his servants do not fight.[26]

At this point Fox and the other Quaker leaders around him began to draw the line more sharply between their burgeoning movement and the last gasps of a failed Commonwealth. The usually unsinkable Fox entered a ten-week state of "travail"[27] during which he withdrew to a Friend's home in Reading. His reaction suggests how deeply he grieved for the passing of England's "day of visitation." The early Quaker peace witness, deeply immersed in the spirituality of the cross, may also be described as a tragic sense of the human condition and of history in general, which I have explored elsewhere.[28]

The resort by a few Friends to the violent option at the end of the 1650s, and even into the 1660s, has led some modern scholars to doubt whether Friends of the first decade were really pacifists and whether Fox's statements spoke for all Friends. Certainly, in the revolutionary situation of the 1650s, in a mercurial movement that was still far from having formal membership and disciplined organization, some confusion at critical moments should not surprise us. Rosemary Moore tersely comments that early Friends were not "pacifist in the modern sense."[29] That is, they did not espouse a generalized ethical philosophy that they hoped everyone would adopt as reasonable and serving the general good. It would be more adequate to say that early Friends held their testimony against violence as part of a profoundly new birth, a mode of being in the world radically different from the cultural mainstream, reached by way of a desolating deconstruction of the self in the relentless revelation of the light within. Their testimony was no naïve plea to "give peace a chance." It was an apocalyptic unmasking of the machinations of worldly power, corruption, injustice, and violence. As Burrough witnessed, the space of the Lamb's War is found, held, and advanced through revolutionary patience and suffering.

A Post-Revolutionary Quaker Peace Testimony

Given their sense of betrayal by the army and Parliament in the 1650s, early Friends were not entirely aggrieved to see the restoration of monarchy. They viewed it as God's judgment upon a Puritan regime gone wrong. Several, including Fox, published letters of greeting to Charles II at the time of his coronation in June 1660, promising to live peaceably under the new government. Among them, Margaret Fell, a close ally of Fox in the north of England, published *A Declaration and an Information from us the People of God called Quakers* to the king and both houses of Parliament during the week of the coronation. She wished to interpret their principles to Charles, who had only recently entered the country from exile in Holland. Despite cruel treatment by several provisional governments in the past eight years, "We bear our Testimony against all Strife, and Wars, and Contentions."[30] She asserted that "we desire and expect liberty of conscience and just rights and outward liberties as we've been promised by the King."[31]

Indeed, before entering England, Charles had proposed a tolerant religious policy (in his Declaration of Breda). Fell promised that Friends would love, own, and honor the king and his government *so far as* the latter ruled for God's truth and did not impose upon freedom of conscience. This was not a threat of rebellion but a promise of civil disobedience to unjust laws, particularly any regarding religious freedom, which Friends viewed as the driving force for civil liberties and social reform generally. Fell's tract was endorsed by Fox and twelve other male leaders in the movement.

Nevertheless, when Fifth Monarchists attempted another armed insurrection the following January, some 4,230 Quakers were rounded up and jailed by a new Restoration regime with little interest in parsing one radical sect's politics from another's. Fox managed to remain at large in London, and he met with another leader, Richard Hubberthorne, to draft and publish a stronger and more categorical peace statement. This document, known in Quaker tradition as "The 1660 Declaration," is one of the great corporate peace statements in history. Its opening paragraph is worth quoting in full:

> Our principle is, and our practices have always been, to seek peace and ensue it and to follow after righteousness and the knowledge of God, seeking the good and welfare and doing that which tends to the peace of all. We know that wars and fightings proceed from the lusts of men (as Jas. iv. 1–3), out of which lusts the Lord hath redeemed us, and so out of the occasion of war. The occasion of which war, and war itself (wherein envious men, who are lovers of themselves more than lovers of God, lust, kill, and desire to have men's lives or estates) ariseth from the lust. All bloody principles and practices, we, as to our own particulars, do utterly deny, with all outward wars and strife and fightings with outward weapons, for any end or under any pretence whatsoever. And this is our testimony to the whole world.[32]

Again, the deeper spiritual sources of war are prominently stated and vehemently renounced by early Friends, who have been "redeemed" from them by God's power. This acute perspective allows them to deny war and violence "as to our particulars"—as for themselves. Again, this is not an ethical philosophy, not even a religious philosophy, but an existential testimony.

Hence, they stand at some distance from the rest of society, which has not come into "obedience to God's truth." They can only wait for others to come to the same degree of surrender to divine will:

> As for the kingdoms of this world, we cannot covet them, much less can we fight for them, but we do earnestly desire and wait, that by the Word of God's power and its effectual operation in the hearts of men, the kingdoms of this world may become the kingdoms of the Lord, and of his Christ [see Revelation 11:15], that he may rule and reign in men by his spirit and truth, that thereby all people, out of all different judgements and professions may be brought into love and unity with God, and with one another, and that they may all come to witness the prophet's words who said, "Nation shall not lift up sword against nation, neither shall they learn war any more" (Isa. ii. 4; Mic. iv. 3).[33]

In the previous decade, Friends may have expected that England would soon become the kingdom of God. But that day had passed; Fox and Hubberthorne write here with a more cautious—and less revolutionary—voice. They go on to repeat earlier affirmations that civil authority has a legitimate role, to which they will be subject. Reviewing the past eight years, Friends "have not made resistance against authority, but wherein we could not obey for conscience' sake, we have suffered even the most of any people in the nation."[34]

The language of spiritual warfare, so strong in the previous decade, is muted but still significant: "Our weapons are spiritual and not carnal, yet mighty through God to the plucking down of the strongholds of

Satan who is author of wars, fighting, murder and plots."[35] The countercultural practices of Friends would continue to confront and question violent and unjust social norms, although less aggressively than before. Warnings to persecutors are also moderated: "O friends offend not the Lord and his little ones, neither afflict his people . . . but mind and consider mercy, justice, and judgement; that is the way for you to prosper and get the favour of the Lord."[36] God's left hand will bless civil powers that do not afflict those in the right hand.

Moore finds the document to be rather "economical with the truth," given the defections of the previous decade (noted above). Moreover, Fox and the other eleven signers of the statement were in no position to bind the entire loosely organized movement to their assertions. But Fox remained central to the movement, owing in part to his ability to define and encourage its overall tendency in this and other matters.[37]

Shifts in Context and Content

The profile of the movement from 1660 to 1666 shifted from revolutionary to *resistant*. Quaker demands for social reform and provocative public actions were greatly reduced. Still, Friends were prime targets of a Cavalier Parliament bent on punishing and repressing radicals who had frustrated the designs of England's "natural rulers" for two decades. The Quaker Act of 1662 made gatherings of five or more Friends illegal. The Conventicle Act of 1665 generalized the ban to include all nonconforming groups. Unlike other groups, however, Quakers stubbornly continued to hold their meetings openly at regular times and places, inviting mass arrest and imprisonment. Their meticulous record-keeping of their sufferings under persecution may have been inspired in part by the suggestion in Revelation 6:11 that a certain number of martyrdoms would precipitate divine judgment against persecutors.

More strategically, however, Friends used these statistics in publications and petitions to heap public shame upon the government's policies and encourage moderation. In either case, it would appear that Friends still hoped for aid from the left hand of providence.

The Restoration weathered some jolting left jabs from providence: plague in 1664–65, the Great Fire of London in 1666, and a devastating sneak attack by the Dutch upon the British fleet in early 1667. Fire, plague, and sword; these were judgments with biblical resonance. But meanwhile, persecution was killing off key leaders in the movement. Leaders who were still alive and not in prison began shifting the profile of the movement from resistance to *counter-restoration*. A more organized and coherent Quaker body could survive a hostile environment and preserve its countercultural faith and practice against the anti-utopian backlash of Restoration England.

After two years of harsh imprisonment in Lancaster and Scarborough castles, Fox emerged in September 1666 (the day the Great Fire of London began, as he recalls it) to undertake a major organizational initiative, in concert with other surviving leaders. He noted that many persecutors had risen and fallen over the past fourteen years, but "the Lord . . . hedged his lambs about and did preserve them on eagles' wings."[38] That is, persecution had served God's purposes left-handedly, making the movement's boundaries more distinct. Fox's work was now to strengthen the "hedge": "the Lord opened to me and let me see what I must do, and how I must order and establish the Men's and Women's Monthly and Quarterly Meetings in all the nation." The reference to "eagles' wings" echoes Exodus 19:4–6, where the Lord calls Israel a "treasured possession," a "peculiar people" whom God had carried on eagles' wings. The covenant-sealing moment in Quaker development had arrived. It was a covenant sealed with the blood of Quaker martyrs.

Fox understood the Spirit-led business practices of men's and women's meetings to be a peaceful "restoration by Christ, into the image of God, and his righteousness and holiness again, in that they are helps-meet, man and woman, as they were before the fall."[39] Counter to the restored monarchy of Charles II, heir to the throne,

> Every man and woman that be heirs of the Gospel, they are heirs of this authority and the power of God. . . . So they come to inherit and possess . . . the power of God which will last for ever and outlast all the orders of the devil and all that is set up of men or by men.[40]

Like the children of Israel coming into the promised land, Fox exhorts Friends to inhabit more fully and coherently the social space they had begun to establish in the Lamb's War of the 1650s. Again, this is the realm of Christ's government, amid but not of the realm of Charles II or any government to come. The world outside this hedged garden might continue to be a hostile wilderness, but this peculiar people would "take care of God's glory"[41] by modeling a blameless and holy life, drawing others who still yearned for the kingdom of heaven on earth.

This crucial juncture in Quaker history established the basic pattern of Quaker faith and practice for the next 150 years. As Friends organized for a longer-term future, *peace still found the purpose of a peculiar people*. Friends certainly appeared to be a *peculiar people*, in the worldly sense, to their neighbors. An anti-Quaker tract published anonymously in 1678 by Thomas Comber, an Anglican priest, described Friends as unified mainly by distinctively annoying behaviors he described as "shibboleths": "touch not, taste not, handle not." He identified the origins of these peculiar manners (such as the plain dress and language of "thee" and "thou") in the radical politics of the Civil War decade, particularly the levelling principles of Gerrard

Winstanley. He concluded that Quaker faith and practices were "the most Damnable and pernitious an Heresy, as hath assaulted Christianity at any time."[42]

Certainly by 1678, the initial, revolutionary outburst of Quaker witness was being integrated into a coherent set of Christian convictions, forged by a powerful interaction of spiritual experience and material practices. Quakers had become a coherent people, peculiarly God's. Theirs was of course not the only way to live a moral and holy life. But the *coherence* of their collective practices communicated to the wider society, much as Jesus had told his followers their community would shine like "a city set upon a hill" (Matthew 5:14). Such coherence, forged within a particular social context, is necessarily idiosyncratic—odd, peculiar.

These practices continued to develop through the peaceful means of personal and collective processes of spiritual discernment. The continuing discipline of surrender to God and one another in these practices made Quaker group processes the preeminent form of peace testimony in this post-revolutionary period. The shift of perspective from an *eschatological* end-time framed by the Book of Revelation to a *protological* restoration of Eden, framed by the opening chapters of Genesis, shifted Quaker energies from a revolutionary conflict with the Puritan establishment to an intensified engagement with the creation. This found expression in a striking Quaker élan in business, in new sciences and technologies, and in migration to the Edenic wilderness of the New World. Quaker religious practices meshed with their socioeconomic practices in ways that are difficult for contemporary Friends to grasp in today's more secularized society, where religious life is largely individualized and bracketed off from economic and other social realms. Thus, *peace found new purposes among a peculiar people*. In essence, the purpose remained to "take care of God's glory," but that played out in a wide variety of concrete, material directions. The creative genius of Quaker faith and practice in this period is hard to overstate. As a people still under official persecution in England until 1689, and still religious pariahs long after that, the generative power of the emerging Religious Society of Friends was vast.

Some of the valences of this second period are demonstrated by two key second-generation leaders, Robert Barclay and William Penn. We will examine mainly the ways they advanced the reframing of the peace testimony that began with the "1660 Declaration."

Robert Barclay, a Presbyterian, university-educated member of the Scottish gentry, was convinced in 1666, the year Fox initiated his counter-restoration program among Friends. Barclay's short life ended in 1690, at age forty-two. He served as an absentee governor of the Quaker-dominated colony of East Jersey. But his main contributions to the Quaker movement were theological, particularly his *Apology for the True Christian Divinity* (1678), a robust defense of his newly adopted faith. A brilliant treatise, it defines and defends Quaker faith and practice using the framework of the Presbyterian Westminster Catechism of Faith. That theological framework inevitably neutralized the apocalyptic, revolutionary witness of the first generation. But Barclay had Fox's blessing and encouragement in the project, which made Friends more intelligible to Christians who viewed them from very different presuppositions.

Barclay's treatment of the peace testimony comes under the *Apology's* fifteenth and final proposition. He develops his argument well, using texts not only from the New Testament but also from early Church fathers to make a strong case for the pacifism of early Christians. Turning to present circumstances, he anticipates the objection that Christians must obey magistrates who command them to defend their country. He responds that if a magistrate is a true Christian, he will not command military service. If he is not a true Christian and commands it, then true

Christians must obey their lord and true king, Jesus Christ, and resist military service. He adds that the refusal of violence is

> the most perfect part of the Christian religion, as that wherein the denial of self and entire confidence in God doth most appear, and therefore Christ and his apostles left us hereof a most perfect example. . . . [However, seeing that most Christians] have not come to the pure dispensation of the Gospel, and therefore, while they are in that condition, we shall not say that war, undertaken upon a just occasion, is altogether unlawful to them . . . so the present confessors of the Christian name, who are yet in the mixture, and not in the patient suffering spirit, are not yet fitted for this form of Christianity, and therefore cannot be undefending themselves, until they attain that perfection.[43]

Thus, Barclay extends the logic first articulated by Fox and Hubberthorne in January 1661, even to the point of providing a "just war" theology for those still "in the mixture" of Christian faith and civil imperatives. But he retains the Quaker conviction that true Christian divinity is "the patient suffering spirit" that can and will refuse war. First-generation Friends had hoped and even expected to *sacralize* all of society through their sacrificial, revolutionary witness. They hoped to draw all into the kingdom of heaven on earth through their preaching and their lived testimony. Now, in this new phase, they perfected a hedged, *sectarian* faith and practice within a society whose *secularizing* processes were accelerating.[44] Other churches might make various compromises between Christian faith and state imperatives, but Friends would continue to defend this socio-spiritual space with their lives, in both living and dying.

The peace testimony was born of Quaker end-time consciousness in the 1650s. It remained an absolute commitment among Friends but was becoming relative externally in the meantime world, where Friends felt compelled to tolerate cultural Christianity if they hoped to be tolerated in return. Barclay articulated the post-revolutionary mode of the peace testimony as a prophetic refusal of military service and of war-related commerce, alongside a conciliatory recognition that others did not share the radical faith attained by Friends.

William Penn, another upper-class convert to Friends (in 1666–67), furthered this two-track logic with visionary proposals for limiting interstate violence. His *Essay towards the Present and Future Peace of Europe* (1693) built upon the Dutch-brokered Treaty of Westphalia (1648) that had already begun to wind down the protracted warfare of the sixteenth and early seventeenth centuries. Penn pointed out the enormous liabilities of war vis-à-vis human welfare and the economic progress of nations. But he also realistically appealed to the aristocratic viewpoint of ruling dynasties that were likely to dominate Europe for the foreseeable future. Penn proposed a "diet" (parliament) of European states to settle international disputes and establish international law. The diet would allow only small military forces to be kept by each state. No single state would be powerful enough to dominate the others.

Historian of pacifism Peter Brock notes that Penn's proposals presaged the present-day European Union and constituted the first major initiative of an activist Quaker peace testimony. "But for Friends, for the 'people of God' (as some Quakers liked to call themselves), a different rule held. It was the one compactly expressed by Penn when he said, 'not fighting, but suffering' was the evidence of their peace testimony."[45]

Brock describes Penn's *Essay* as a pragmatic program to attain some degree of peace until the coming of the Peaceable Kingdom. But both Penn and Barclay remained clear regarding the distinction between the peace testimony as a prophetic renunciation of violence by a gathered people and their wider efforts to limit violence in the world at large.[46]

The Peace Testimony in Colonial America

That distinction was reconfigured in American colonies where Friends dominated government. In that role, they were obligated to wield "the magistrate's sword" to some extent. Their attempt to balance the right and left hands of God was soon tested. The first test came in Rhode Island, a colony founded by Baptists and other dissenters from Massachusetts. But Friends had grown rapidly there and had come to dominate the government in the late seventeenth century. They inherited deteriorating relations with Native American tribes, however, and were confronted in 1676–77 with the crisis of King Philip's War, an Indian uprising against colonial settlers. The Quaker-led government responded by first granting the right of conscientious objection to military service, then raising a militia to defend against attacking tribes.[47]

In the colony of West Jersey, Quaker leaders produced a progressive constitution but were soon overwhelmed by non-Quaker elements in the 1670s. They never really had the opportunity to work out a Quaker vision of colonial life.

These compromised experiments informed William Penn's colonial strategy when he received the charter for Pennsylvania in 1680. Penn drew large numbers of Friends from England and Wales and actively advertised Pennsylvania among Mennonites and other persecuted sects on the Continent. His efforts produced a colonial government strongly dominated by Friends and supported by a bloc of quietist religious groups for the next seventy years. Moreover, by setting a peaceful and respectful tone with Native peoples from the outset, Friends were able to avert territorial conflicts. They managed without a militia. Penal codes were softened; murder was the only capital offense, in contrast to sixteen capital offenses in Massachusetts at the time.

Penn described his colony variously as the "Fifth Kingdom" (alluding to the biblical prophecies of Daniel), the "Day of Christ," and a "Holy Experiment." It was indeed one of the most audacious political initiatives in history. Just as we grossly underestimate the first generation of Friends when we describe them as starting a new religious denomination, so we distort Penn's efforts when we frame Pennsylvania as one of thirteen colonies that converged in the founding of the United States. Powerful utopian impulses underlay the religious and political efforts of early Friends. The military victory of the American Revolution was the final defeat of a far greater vision of what Pennsylvania and America might have been. It lies beyond the scope of this essay to explore adequately the Quaker experience in Pennsylvania. But it is worth briefly noting Jane Calvert's recent study[48] of the spiritual politics of Penn's vision and the evolution of the Quaker colony.

One salient point of Calvert's study of Penn's political thought adds a helpful perspective to our concern for the Quaker peace testimony and its significance today. Penn framed an understanding of civil society and its constitutional basis that was extrapolated from the early Quaker understanding of the Church. He argued that divine sovereignty resides properly in the people. The constitution of a civil society is a living reality, evolving among the people themselves. It is God's law, discerned dimly but progressively through collective political processes. Rather than use Quaker religious terms like "light" and "discernment," Penn drew upon a philosophical term going back to Plato, *synteresis*, to denote the intuitive manner in which God's law is perceived in the human conscience.

A written constitution is not the living constitution that dwells among the people but only a provisional declaration of it.[49] Like the Quaker understanding of Scripture, it is not the fountain of divine revelation but a historic expression of it. The written constitution is a contract that is in a process of continual negotiation (in fact, Penn's initial constitution for Pennsylvania went through twenty years of resistance and revision before it was finally adopted). The living constitution continues to find further clarification in written law through the interaction of two key principles: the integrity and perpetuity of the constitution and the peaceful processes of dissent and advocacy for rights. Both principles must be faithfully and vigorously maintained in creative tension for the constitution to remain healthy and progressive.

Calvert adopts the sailing metaphor of "trimming" to describe this principle. The weight of a sailboat's crew must be shifted and re-shifted toward one side of the boat and then the other, not kept in the middle. Hence, the political process is not maintained by settling on one side or the other, or by resting in a supposedly happy mean, but by a constant, skillful shifting of weight/emphasis/advocacy between concern for order and stability on the one hand and a destabilizing drive for reform on the other. Isaac Penington, first-generation Friend and father-in-law of Penn, may have influenced Penn's political theories. Penington appears to draw upon the "trimming" metaphor in a 1651 tract on political order:

> It becometh everyone (both in reference to himself and the whole) to contribute his utmost towards the right steering of this Vessel towards the preserving of it both in its state and motions.[50]

The logic of "trimming" informs the peace testimony in conversation with civil power, which can at times appear contradictory, hypocritical or cynically pragmatic. But once understood, it defines a politics that can be radically pacifist and stridently oppositional but at the same time uphold the coercive power and evolving integrity of civil government. Calvert's insights go far to answer Meredith Weddle's conclusions to her study of the Rhode Island Quaker solution to King Philip's War. Notwithstanding her excellent investigation of that case, Weddle is perplexed by the "intractable incoherence of the peace testimony," "a dramatic contradiction" between early Friends' testimony renouncing war and their testimony concerning government's duty to restrain evil.[51]

Calvert argues that the Quaker practice of civil disobedience, which had already been evolving for thirty years by the time Penn drafted his first constitution, embodied these twin principles. Even in its most revolutionary expressions, the Lamb's War challenged unjust laws openly and peacefully, with willingness to suffer the consequences, in faithfulness to the constitutional integrity of the state no matter how flawed its legal expression. Calvert views Friends as key early modern practitioners of civil disobedience and their colonial experiments as an underrated influence on subsequent American political history.

Before proceeding further, it is worth noting briefly the thought of Jim Corbett, American Quaker political theorist and a key initiator of the Sanctuary Movement to provide safe haven for Central American political refugees in the 1980s. Corbett preferred the term civil *initiative* over civil disobedience.[52] He found the latter term overly oppositional in tone. The Sanctuary Movement, for example, broke and challenged federal laws against harboring illegal aliens. When brought to trial, Corbett and the other defendants argued that they were simply enacting the international law of the Nuremberg principles, which require not only governments but individuals to protect political refugees. In providing for refugees, the network of Sanctuary churches and synagogues thus enacted the human rights provisions the federal government was pledged and obligated to perform but was instead contravening. Corbett's example and rationale exemplifies the "trimming" ethic of Friends: breaking an unjust and inhumane policy of the government in order to promote a greater level of fidelity to its actual constitution.

The example of the Sanctuary Movement also highlights the role of sectarian groups in pressing moral and social concerns in the evolving constitution of civil society. The soul-searching and moral principles of religious groups intensify the process of *synteresis* in civil society, which can be severely compromised by nationalism, racism, and the corrosive influences of a market economy. Or, to return to the image of the two hands of providence, sectarian groups keep working to draw the left and right hands of God closer together.

Britain's imperial war policies in America finally forced Friends to begin withdrawing from political leadership in Pennsylvania in the 1750s. The French and Indian (or Seven Years') War forced an enlargement of "the magistrate's sword" in Pennsylvania that became an outright contradiction to the peace testimony.[53] But even as Friends withdrew from political leadership, they worked as quiet advocates on both sides of the Atlantic for reconciliation between Britain and the colonies in the years leading up to the American Revolution.[54] After violent instigators in Massachusetts pitched the conflict into military action in 1775, Friends were increasingly stigmatized as "loyalists." The Quaker experiment with peaceful political power came to an end. Their political influence greatly diminished as Friends were relegated to the margins of American life by 1800.

Yet the faithfulness of Friends to the advancement of the constitution of civil society continued through their political advocacy on behalf of Native American tribes, their renunciation of slaveholding, their pathbreaking work to end the slave trade, and many other instances of prophetic opposition and political advocacy. British Friend Grigor McClelland[55] distilled the "trimming" logic of Friends into the paradigm of "prophets and reconcilers." The prophetic Quaker mode (so dominant in the first generation) takes an absolute position demanding peace and justice, whereas the reconciling mode (given classic expression in Penn's *Essay for the Peace of Europe*) works to bridge the conflicting interests of different parties in conflict in order to find pragmatic solutions to specific conflicts. The prophetic mode stands fast in the suffering ethic that both Penn and Barclay maintained for the people of God (in God's right hand), whereas the reconciling mode moves more pragmatically (with less acute suffering but great patience) in the confusing mix of violent and nonviolent, just and unjust parties (ever jostling in God's left hand).

Of course, there have been many permutations of the Quaker peace testimony in Britain and America since 1800, in conversation with the evolving (sometimes devolving) constitution of modern society. Peter Brock's works on the history of pacifism in general and among Friends in particular are important resources.[56] But, for the purposes of this essay, perhaps it is adequate to stop here, having sketched the basic dynamics of Quaker peacemaking during its first 150 years. It remains for us to consider the implications of our study for the Quaker peace testimony in this new century.

Part 3

Peace Still Finds the Purpose of a Peculiar People Today

As suggested at the start of this essay, the diffuse identity and weakened commitment of Friends pose dilemmas for the Quaker peace testimony today. We no longer strive to be a peculiar people. Under these conditions the peace testimony easily becomes doctrinaire, a proliferating set of views regarding foreign policy, militarism, gun laws, etc. However well taken and strongly expressed, these opinions and advocacies too easily fall short of existential commitments.

The light within, which gave early and traditional Friends such conviction, becomes an inner light, the source of freely adopted subjective viewpoints. A vague notion of "continuing revelation" is used reflexively by Friends to shrug off uncomfortable truths from past generations of Friends and to make any current faith and practice subject to perpetual revision. Continuing revelation becomes a continuing reservation. But the traditional Quaker belief in continuing revelation emphasizes the light's *consistency*, not its changeability. The light shows us how to remain faithful amid changing circumstances; it doesn't discard older revelations as if tearing off the pages of a calendar.

Behind these phenomena lies the tendency of liberal Friends to read the values of civil society into the Religious Society of Friends. To be sure, the plurality of experience and ethics of a healthy civil society, with universal rights guaranteed by a constitution, are to be cherished and actively advanced by Friends as citizens. But the Religious Society of Friends is not a subset of civil society. It is a religious society with a corporate, historic set of understandings and commitments to God and to one another. It is a covenantal body, not a constitutional one. A covenantal community is bound together in shared understandings and commitments. But that binding simultaneously separates us from those who may have sympathies and affinities with us but are not willing to share our commitments (see the reflections on the meaning of covenant in the Hebrew tradition in the essay on the other side of this book). They may be happier in another religious group or at large in secular, civil society, which is to be respected. Friends have no monopoly on truth and integrity.

Civil society functions best as a religiously and morally neutral realm that maintains space for various groups, each with their own freely chosen commitments, and for individuals without such commitments. Civil society creates a healthy, pluralistic context for religious bodies, just as religious bodies contribute to the health and progress of civil society. As noted earlier in this essay, civil society exercises a certain degree of coercive power ("the magistrate's sword") in order to maintain some minimal definitions of peace and justice, a baseline from which individuals and groups can work for social betterment.

Recall Penn's concept of the civil constitution as a living reality that exists among the people. In whatever ways they might describe it, most people in civil society possess an implicit sense of that living constitution. They work to improve it through political processes of discernment and dialogue Penn called *synteresis*. Through official political mechanisms and social processes too various to define, the civil constitution of society either advances or corrupts. Religious groups and other forms of civil association are important catalysts in that process.

A healthy and renewed Quaker peace testimony must reorient itself to the specific identity and purpose of a religious society within civil society. Today, however, our collective identity and sense of purpose are increasingly Balkanized into a jostling variety of secular categories (race, class, gender, sexuality, subjective religious preferences, etc.). These generate corresponding civil agendas for political advocacy that Friends typically adopt from the wider progressivist sector of civil society.

All these actions are important within a secular, civil frame of reference. But along the way, all four orienting factors (the four Ps) of our Religious Society drift into undefined relationship with one another. Friends have little idea today what it means to be a people in God's right hand. Consequently, we shuffle confusedly among an ever-widening array of entities and identities in God's left-handed and ironic providence. In the final analysis, our presumed modesty in declining to be a people (among others) called and chosen to fulfill divine purposes in the world is a refusal to be a suffering people who find our freedom in submitting to the divine will, collectively discerned.

These criticisms may sound harsh and unfair to many readers. But over the past forty years of active ministry, as I have sojourned in different sectors of Friends in America and Britain, I have observed too many passing enthusiasms and fruitless digressions not to be concerned. The casual participation of many Friends in their meetings today, the white, middle-class mindset that frames most Quaker conversations, the vague wondering-aloud nature of much vocal ministry in meeting for worship, the everybody-gets-a-chance-to-say-something meandering of meetings for business, the recreational style of much social witness—these fill me with misgivings for Friends, especially those of my own baby boom generation. I take some hope in the rumblings I occasionally hear from young adult Friends. But I have seen the complacency that overtook my own generation and fear that some version of the same trajectory may overcome younger Friends as well (please take that as a friendly challenge, my young friends).

But let us return to the theological perspective derived from 1 Peter earlier in this essay and now combine that early Christian witness with its reformulation among early Friends, providing a second historical instance. A triangulation of those two reference points with our present situation may help us to navigate the confusing territory of this young century. How may we map the space of the Quaker peace testimony today, in terms of our "four Ps"? It may be useful to reproduce here the pairing of dialectical pairs charted out earlier.

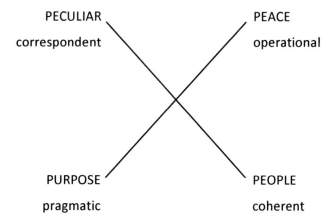

A Peculiar People

First, consider the issues of point of reference and frame of reference, the interaction of personal experience with a shared, coherent set of understandings. Liberal Friends strongly emphasize personal experience as the touchstone of their Quakerism. But that point of reference constantly shifts among the multiple frames of reference that we appropriate from the wider secular culture. We freely trade among humanist, skeptical, Buddhist, Christian, psychological, and scientific frames for our experience. Certainly, we learn something important from each, but the self tends to float indeterminately and without *conviction* among them. And that flux increases exponentially at the group level as we bring these multiple framings to bear in vocal ministry and meetings for business in our local meetings.

As seen earlier, the early Christian and early Quaker movements were strongly countercultural. Their adherents were often considered pariahs. By contrast, liberal renewal in the early twentieth century transformed Friends from "quirky sectarians" into a dynamic fellowship of seekers and social experimenters, as Leigh Eric Schmidt summarizes.[57] The shift from quaint to cosmopolitan has brought with it the admiration and approval of many whom Friends admire. But we have become habituated to middle-class, progressive respectability. We savor every approving word spoken of Quakers. Mildred Binns Young, a Quaker writer who grounded her visionary writings in her subsistence farming with poor black and white families, warned in 1960 that Friends are "bound into a system to which war and poverty are integral."[58] Certainly,

> History is in the hand of God, but within that Hand, man is given freedom and commission to act. . . . Christ was sent to act for God in history; each of us is also sent to act, according

to our measure, for God and for our fellow men.[59]

She asked, "Are Friends fit to answer the summons of our time?"[60] Sadly, Young's social theology was becoming unintelligible and unattractive even then.

The First Letter of Peter invites us to be built around Christ, the living stone, rejected by human builders but chosen and precious to God. For Friends to reclaim Christian faith as our shared frame of reference is not a surrender to the dead hand of tradition. It is a surrender to the hands of the living God, who is not something to be discussed and accepted or rejected but someone active in our lives and in the world, whose thoughts are not always our thoughts, whose will is not always ours. It is indeed a "fearful thing," as the Letter to the Hebrews testifies. But it is ultimately liberating and empowering. It teaches the true meaning of peace.

Biblical Christian faith as a shared frame of reference, a *group* language, does not rule out a variety of *personal* affinities and explorations, religious and social. These enrich our personal journeys and contribute to the life of the group. But without a shared language and group identity, we begin to speak to one another in memes and sound bites too fragmentary to engender a deeper group discernment. We settle for lowest common denominators in decision-making.

Many Friends today would respond that they simply do not have an experience of a living God or an encounter with a living Christ to make such language authentic. But I think of Jim Corbett, a non-theist Friend, whose response to political refugees in the desert of southern Arizona led him into a rich exploration of the Bible with a local Roman Catholic priest and other Christians helping to start the Sanctuary movement. His writings are filled with biblically informed political insights.[61]

Personal faith grows in conversation with others who are also growing in faith, and the dialogue builds a matrix of peoplehood among us. Over time, our shared understandings and commitments become more *peculiar*. Less awash in the crosscurrents of secular culture, we begin to take on a real character and collective personality through the things we feel personally and collectively called to do.

The Quaker "testimonies" are the various words we speak and actions we undertake in consistent ways that express what we feel called to be in the world. We can give them names that have general intelligibility and broad appeal, like "equality," "community," "peace," and so on. But there are unique and peculiar ways in which we are led into them and enact them. As we live more fully into our testimonies, both individually and as a body of Friends, we may seem more peculiar or odd to the secular society around us—but we also become God's "treasured possession," a "peculiar people." What may appear to be a loss of personal freedom to outsiders feels on the inside to be a greater freedom from the conformities of mainstream me-too-ism. It is freedom *for* God and others.

To be sure, Quaker peculiarity is not the only path of integrity and faithfulness in the world. There are other groups in the wider society for us to respect, admire, and collaborate with. Each is idiomatic to its own collective history of faithfulness. Indeed, these other traditions may also be in God's right hand of providence. Each is called in a different way and toward a particular divine purpose, whether or not they would articulate it in those terms. But it does us no good to participate fully in no tradition in order to respect all of them. Our surrender to one of them is our path to God, community, and our truest selves. As William James observed, true religion is an acute fever, not a dull habit.

In becoming a peculiar people, we find ourselves becoming the "aliens and exiles" Peter addresses in his letter. Our critical distance from the jumble of secular identities and lifestyles affords a more discerning perspective on them. Seeing dispassionately past the language, fashions, and moral codes of others, we may see more compassionately into the hearts and the needs of others. This empathetic gaze and the way we act upon it is what Friends have traditionally called "answering that of God in everyone." It's not necessarily finding the "good" in everyone. It may be an insight into the hurt in another person, or the way a person is fighting against God's presence, rebelling against God's love.

We see that more clearly in others once we have recognized it more clearly in ourselves and moved on to surrender and servanthood. We are thrust into compassionate response to others as we "abstain from the works of the flesh" that keep us in competition and conflict. We are free to speak and act not as vying equals but as outsiders with a fresh perspective.

We may "answer that of God in everyone" with words and gestures of kindness, helpful counsel, or sometimes prophetic confrontation. In each case, we are acting as a "holy priesthood," offering "spiritual sacrifices" that mediate God's *shalom* between ourselves and others. This is the beginning of peacemaking. The lessons we learn from these encounters provide insight into the wider challenges of work for peace and justice in the world. I have noticed over the years, among Quaker peace activists I most admire, that their work has developed out of the building blocks of loving interaction, respectful listening, honest confrontation, and a willingness to risk being misunderstood or rejected—even physically abused—for their witness. Peace work of this kind is undertaken in the hope that, "though they malign you as evildoers, they may see your honorable deeds and glorify God on the day of visitation," as Peter writes. We may understand "the day of visitation" in this case as that moment when the hostile party finally "gets it," turns to "that of God" within, or aligns with peace (not necessarily joining our cause).

As we freshly receive the call and follow it together, we can expect new forms of coherence to develop. Our growing diversity in recent decades will be fashioned into a new form of unity. Our renewed faith and practice will rebuild us as living stones around Christ in new architectures that fit the social terrain of this new century. The Quaker testimonies will find fresh idioms of expression.

Peace and Purpose

It is time to shift now into the action-oriented dynamics of means and ends, processes and outcomes. The coherence of a peculiar people emerges not only from personal experiences of calling and shared understandings of those experiences; it is forged also by shared *practices*.

I have suggested elsewhere[62] that Friends need to *answer the queries again*, not just reflect on them. The advices and queries challenge us to examine how we are enacting the Quaker testimonies in our lives. Traditionally, meetings answered the queries together and used the answers to assess "how truth prospered" among them. But in the nineteenth century, as the dress and behavioral codes of Friends seemed more rote and formal than truly communicative of Quaker testimony, Friends meetings stopped answering the queries. Individual Friends were thereby freed to experiment creatively in finding their own ways to live out the testimonies. But by the same token, Quaker ethics retreated into the inviolable realm of private life. Today, Friends would be offended to be queried by their local meeting about their way of life. We thus become less a "peculiar people" than a collection of rather peculiar individuals.

Certainly, a reversion to archaic codes of behavior and to traditional practices of answering the queries would be stultifying to most of us. A renewal of shared practices must begin with small groups that gather at their own initiative to share their experiences and experiments in living more simply and sustainably, dealing with greater integrity in the marketplace, engendering greater equality in the workplace, becoming more creative witnesses for peace, and so on. Candid sharing, nonjudgmental listening, learning from one another's example, encouraging and even challenging one another—these interactions will weave new patterns of Quaker integrity and witness in the world. Some of this already occurs in various networks of Friends, spreading like a plant's rhizomes, connecting around common concerns. But can the standing bodies of Friends again become meaningful sites of renewal?

Renewal in all of these testimonies is a form of peacemaking. For example, living more simply disempowers the forces of envy, emulation, competition, and conflict that fuel violence and war. Living in more sustainable patterns reduces the monstrous violence that humans are wreaking upon the earth. The integrity of courageous, plain speech cuts through the tacit hypocrisy that perpetuates social distance and bigotry among us. It tends to initiate more equitable racial, gendered, and other relations at work and in other spheres. It counters the inflated language of media hype, patriotic jingoism, and warmongering. Work for equality augurs well for economic justice and counters the racial fears that breed violence throughout the fabric of society. Greater equality fosters new forms of community in all kinds of social contexts, while community makes equality more personally real and joyful. Through all these practices, the "peace testimony" becomes much more than a protest against violence at home and abroad. Peace is a proactive, holistic renewal of *shalom*.

As noted earlier, after the Roman Empire embraced Christianity as its official religion, both the pacifism and purpose of the early Church were quickly converted to imperial policy and purposes. It was also noted that the

Anabaptist and early Quaker break with the state-church equation came along with their embrace of nonviolence as an absolute commitment. Their *purpose* was not church growth, but they did spread rapidly. Nor was their purpose equality, justice, or an end to war, but their group ethics and wider social influence moved in those directions. Their only purpose was to "take care of God's glory," as Fox urged, or to "proclaim the mighty acts of him who called you out of darkness into his marvelous light," as 1 Peter expresses it. Yet that made them more creative than a set of well-defined goals would have inspired.

As long as Friends import our identities, ethics, and goals from secular society, we will continue to be doctrinaire about peace and confused about our purpose. Over the past century, our activist impulses have kept us grasping for social relevance rather than living in radical faithfulness where we are and letting the conflicts and talking points develop from the ways we puzzle and offend the mainstream. Answering the call to an otherworldly holiness does not take its cues from the media's hot-button issues. The *process* of living peace will discover our purpose. Standing fast in the truth we have received, the world will come to us with enough conflict. Certainly, we should question whether we are communicating our testimony to the world. But if we conclude that we are not, then we should reconsider our way of living rather than cast about for new causes to champion.

Is this a call to a new quietism? I'm not sure, but if it is, so be it. The so-called "quietist" Friends of the eighteenth century were in fact highly engaged in society. This most sectarian and "hedged" period produced the greatest Quaker innovative leadership in industry, trade, science, and technology, particularly in Britain. In America, there was the "holy experiment" in political leadership in Pennsylvania, the renunciation of slaveholding and beginnings of work for abolition, groundbreaking alliances with Native Americans and advocacy on their behalf, and efforts to avert a violent American Revolution.

The sectarian posture of Friends in this period had a paradoxical effect. They withdrew from the increasingly violent, unjust, and rapacious trends of mainstream Anglo-American culture in order to refine their distinctive countercultural faith and practice; they *stood still* in the midst of the headlong changes in social conditions caused by the industrial revolution in England and colonial expansion in America. The more irrelevant they became, the more their contrast with the wider culture revealed the points of conflict and the prophetic witness they needed to maintain.

Today, too, the world around us will do most of the moving, the activism, the agitation that generates envy, competition, injustice, and war. Standing still in a place of integrity, peace, simplicity, community, and equality is our chief task, the site of our most creative peacemaking. Steadfastly resisting the manifold ways in which the world tempts and coerces us to conform will generate more than enough conflict, witness, civil disobedience, and opportunities to serve.

This is the same challenge Paul presented to the church at Galatia. He called the Galatians to stand courageously in the freedom of their new humanity in Christ rather than busy themselves with being religiously legitimate according to the laws of Moses (and thereby safely legal in the Roman Empire):

> *You foolish Galatians! Who has bewitched you? . . . Did you receive the Spirit by doing the works of the law or by believing what you heard? Are you so foolish? Having started with the Spirit, are you now ending with the flesh? Did you experience so much for nothing? . . . For freedom Christ has set us free. Stand firm, therefore, and do not submit*

again to a yoke of slavery. (Galatians 3:1, 3, 4; 5:1)

The Letter to the Ephesians expands on the theme of standing fast and highlights the ways it leads to nonviolent struggle:

*Finally, be strong in the Lord and in the strength of his power. Put on the whole armor of God, so that you may be able to **stand** against the wiles of the devil. For our struggle is not against enemies of blood and flesh, but against the rulers, against the authorities, against the cosmic powers of this present darkness, against the spiritual forces of evil in the heavenly places. Therefore take up the whole armor of God, so that you may be able to with**stand** on that evil day, and having done everything, to **stand** firm. **Stand** therefore, and fasten the belt of truth around your waist, and put on the breastplate of righteousness. As shoes for your feet put on whatever will make you ready to proclaim the gospel of peace. With all these, take the shield of faith, with which you will be able to quench all the flaming arrows of the evil one. Take the helmet of salvation, and the sword of the Spirit, which is the word of God.* (Ephesians 6:10–17, emphases added)

Together, the people are gathered around Christ; they occupy a space that must be defended daily against the powers of alienation, the "desires of the flesh" that "the evil one" uses as "wiles" to draw them out and as "flaming darts" to attack and subvert that space. To "stand still in the light," in Fox's language, is the spiritual practice that maintains that space and lets the sword of the Spirit discern our boundaries. To "stand firm," in Paul's language, evokes the moral and social practices of the community that refine and defend that space. It is God's power that makes this possible.

Human strength alone simply cannot sustain the rigors of the struggle.

The military imagery in Ephesians evokes to me an image of the phalanx formation of troops utilized so successfully by Alexander the Great. These tightly formed blocks of soldiers could stand against attack on all sides. What is required today is a *militant* Quaker peace witness that can answer the militarized culture around us. "Militant" does not necessarily mean military or violent, but it does mean a willingness to engage in focused, sustained conflict.

In his booklet *Study War Some More (If You Want to Work for Peace.)*,[63] Chuck Fager reflects on his years of activism culminating in his work as director of Quaker House in Fayetteville, North Carolina, near the Fort Bragg U.S. Army base. Fager draws lessons from Sun Tzu's ancient treatise, *The Art of War,* and from what he observes of modern military strategy. He suggests that Friends should learn from the military's focused, sustained intention if we hope to counter today's military-industrial complex. Like the military, we need to think long-term and big-picture rather than simply react to the latest outbreak of war. Some of these points will be taken up in the essay on the other side of this book.

But with regard to the internal dynamics of a peace people, Fager makes some points consonant with this essay's emphasis. He emphasizes that a renewed peace testimony must be undergirded by serious study of our own history and of the Bible, greater financial support for our peacemaking organizations, including our local meetings, and a commitment to teaching the art of peacemaking to the next generations. The current Quaker phobia of the Christian Right and obsession with Washington politics too often distract Friends from the urgent tasks the military would call "securing our base."

This refocusing of our energies is essential if we are to make "anti-war" a noun, a substantive counter to warmaking and not simply an adjective describing our reactive stance today.

But it is time now to turn this book (and the standpoint of this essay) upside down and backwards in order to confront the "cosmic powers of this present darkness," where militarism reigns, where authoritarian religion justifies its insatiable demands, and where a pervasive anxiety for security disciplines the citizenry into submission. The essay on the other side of this book draws upon the Book of Revelation, and the early Quaker reading of it, to gain a fresh perspective on this present darkness and to draw fresh insights for a renewed Quaker peace testimony.

NOTES

[1] See Jenifer May Hampton, "British Quaker Survey: Examining Religious Beliefs and Practices in the Twenty-First Century," *Quaker Studies* 19, no. 1 (September 2014): 7–136. On the convergence question, see p. 29. Similar trends may be found among North American Friends.

[2] John H. Elliott, *Conflict, Community, and Honor: 1 Peter in Social-Scientific Perspective* (Eugene, OR: Cascade, 2007).

[3] Wayne A. Meeks, *The First Urban Christians: The Social World of the Apostle Paul* (New Haven: Yale University Press, 1983).

[4] Elliott, *Conflict, Community, and Honor*, 73.

[5] Unless otherwise noted, all quotes from Scripture are taken from the New Revised Standard Version (NRSV) of the Bible.

[6] For more about ancient Roman perceptions, see Robert L. Wilken, *The Christians as the Romans Saw Them* (New Haven: Yale, 1984).

[7] See Douglas Gwyn, "Enacting Truth: The Dynamics of Quaker Practice," *Quaker Theology* 17 (Spring-Summer 2010): 15–47; Douglas Gwyn, *Personality and Place: The Life and Times of Pendle Hill* (Philadelphia: Plain Press, 2014), 446–51.

[8] For more on pre-Quaker groups, including Seekers, see Douglas Gwyn, *Seekers Found: Atonement in Early Quaker Experience* (Wallingford, PA: Pendle Hill Publications, 2000).

[9] For more on these more general developments, see Gwyn, *Seekers Found*; Gwyn, *Apocalypse of the Word: The Life and Message of George Fox* (Richmond, IN: Friends United Press, 2014).

[10] Thomas Edwards, *Gangraena* (1646), as quoted in Gwyn, *Seekers*, 214–15.

[11] George Fox, *Journal of George Fox*, ed. John L. Nickalls (Cambridge: Cambridge University Press, 1952), 65.

[12] George Fox, *To All That Would Know the Way to the Kingdom* (1653), in *The Works of George Fox* (Philadelphia: Gould, 1831), 4: 17–18.

[13] Ibid., 4:22.

[14] Ibid., 4:18.

[15] Fox, Epistle #9, in Fox, *Works*, 7:20.

[16] For a reconstruction of this nonviolent revolutionary agenda, see Douglas Gwyn, *The Covenant Crucified: Quakers and the Rise of Capitalism* (Wallingford, PA: Pendle Hill Publications, 1995).

[17] See Fox, *Journal*, ed. Nickalls, 176.

[18] Ibid., 197–98.

[19] Ibid., 198.

[20] Ibid., 194.

[21] Edward Burrough, *A Measure of the Times* (1657), 34–35, as quoted in Rosemary Moore, *The Light in Their Consciences: The Early Quakers in Britain, 1646–1666* (University Park: Pennsylvania State University Press, 2000), 79–80.

[22] Fox, *Journal*, ed. Nickalls, 354.

[23] George Fox, *To the Councill of Officers of the Armie, and the Heads of the Nation, and for the Inferior Officers and Souldiers to read* (1659), 8. This tract was not republished in later collections of Fox's writings, perhaps indicating that the revolutionary logic of the early Quaker peace testimony was soon lost on later generations.

[24] Ibid.

[25] Ibid.

[26] Fox, *Journal*, ed. Nickalls, 357.

[27] Ibid., 353.

[28] See Douglas Gwyn, "The Early Quaker Lamb's War: Secularization and the Death of Tragedy in Early Modern England," in *Towards Tragedy/Reclaiming Hope: Literature, Theology and Sociology in Conversation*, by Pink Dandelion, Douglas Gwyn, Rachel Muers, Brian Phillips, and Richard E. Sturm (Aldershot, Hampshire, England: Ashgate, 2004), 33–56.

[29] Moore, *The Light in Their Consciences*, 124.

[30] Margaret Fell, *A Declaration and an Information from us the People of God called Quakers, to the Present Governors, the King and Both Houses of Parliament, and to all whom it may Concern* (London, 1660), 7.

[31] Ibid.

[32] Fox, *Journal*, ed. Nickalls, 399. This is a slightly edited version of the text. For the complete text, see *Historical Writings of Quakers against War*, ed. Licia Kuenning (Glenside, PA: Quaker Heritage Press, 2002), 181–88.

[33] Fox, *Journal*, ed. Nickalls, 400.

[34] Ibid., 401.

[35] Ibid., 402.

[36] Ibid.

[37] Moore, *The Light in Their Consciences*, 124, 181.

[38] Fox, *Journal*, ed. Nickalls, 504.

[39] Fox, Epistle #291, in *Works*, 8:39.

[40] Fox, *The Journal of George Fox*, ed. Norman Penney (Cambridge: Cambridge University Press, 1911), 2:128. This was reprinted in part in Fox, *Journal*, ed. Nickalls, 528.

[41] Fox, *Journal*, ed. Nickalls, 511.

[42] Anonymous [Thomas Comber], *Christianity No Enthusiasm* (London, 1678), 6–7, and the closing sentence of "Epistle to the Reader."

[43] Robert Barclay, *Apology for the True Christian Divinity* (1678), (Glenside, PA: Quaker Heritage Press, 2002), 475–76.

[44] For more on secularization in seventeenth-century England, see Charles J. Sommerville, *The Secularisation of Early Modern England: From Religious Culture to Religious Faith* (Oxford: Oxford University Press, 1992). I draw on his work in Gwyn, "The Early Quaker Lamb's War."

[45] Peter Brock, *The Quaker Peace Testimony, 1660–1914* (York, England: Sessions Books, 1990), 86.

[46] Brock, *The Quaker Peace Testimony*, 80, 86.

[47] For an exploration of the Rhode Island Quaker experience, see Meredith Baldwin Weddle, *Walking in the Way of Peace: Quaker Pacifism in the Seventeenth Century* (Oxford: Oxford University Press, 2001).

[48] Jane Calvert, *Quaker Constitutionalism and the Political Thought of John Dickenson* (Cambridge: Cambridge University Press, 2009).

[49] See ibid., 68–89.

[50] Isaac Penington, *Right, Safety and Liberty* (London, 1651), 7, as quoted in Calvert, *Quaker Constitutionalism*, 98.

[51] Weddle, *Walking in the Way of Peace*, 225, 228–29.

[52] Jim Corbett, *Goatwalking* (New York: Viking, 1991), chap. 6.

[53] See Calvert, *Quaker Constitutionalism*, chaps. 3–5; Richard Bauman, *For the Reputation of Truth: Politics, Religion, and Conflict among the Pennsylvania Quakers, 1750–1800* (Baltimore: Johns Hopkins University Press, 1971).

[54] See Arthur J. Mekeel, *The Quakers and the American Revolution* (York, England: Sessions Book Trust, 1996).

[55] Grigor McClelland, "The Prophet and the Reconciler," in *Endeavours to Mend: Perspectives on British Quaker Work in the World Today*, ed. Brian Phillips and John Lampen (London: Quaker Books, 2006), 25–33.

[56] In particular, see Brock, *The Quaker Peace Testimony*; Peter Brock and Nigel Young, *Pacifism in the Twentieth Century* (Toronto: Toronto University Press, 1999).

[57] Leigh Eric Schmidt, *Restless Souls: The Making of American Spirituality* (San Francisco: Harper, 2005), 235.

[58] Mildred Binns Young, *Another Will Gird You: A Message to the Society of Friends*, Pendle Hill Pamphlet #109 (Wallingford, PA: Pendle Hill Publications, 1960), 2.

[59] Ibid., 4.

Endnotes

[60] Ibid., 7. For more on Young's life and writings, see Gwyn, *Personality and Place*.

[61] Besides the aforementioned *Goatwalking*, see Corbett's two Pendle Hill Pamphlets, *The Sanctuary Church*, Pamphlet #270 (Wallingford, PA: Pendle Hill Publications, 1986); and, with Ricardo Elford, *The Servant Church*, Pamphlet #328 (Wallingford, PA: Pendle Hill Publications, 1996).

[62] Douglas Gwyn, *A Sustainable Life: Quaker Faith and Practice in the Renewal of Creation* (Philadelphia: Quaker Press, 2014).

[63] Chuck Fager, *Study War Some More (If You Want to Work for Peace.)* (Fayetteville, NC: Quaker House, 2010).

Works Cited for the Entire Book

Alexander, Michelle. *The New Jim Crow: Mass Incarceration in the Age of Color Blindness*. New York: New Press, 2012.

Anonymous [Thomas Comber]. *Christianity No Enthusiasm*. London, 1678.

Arrighi, Giovanni. *The Long Twentieth Century: Money, Power and the Origins of Our Times*. New York: Verso, 1994.

Badiou, Alain. Saint Paul: *The Foundation of Universalism*. Palo Alto: Stanford University Press, 2003.

Barbour, Hugh, and Arthur Roberts, eds. *Early Quaker Writings, 1650–1700*. Grand Rapids: Eerdmans, 1973.

Barclay, Robert. *Apology for the True Christian Divinity (1678)*. Glenside, PA: Quaker Heritage Press, 2002.

Barnet, Richard J., and Ronald E. Muller. *Global Reach: The Power of the Multinational Corporations*. New York: Simon & Schuster, 1974.

Bauckham, Richard. *The Climax of Prophecy: Studies on the Book of Revelation*. Edinburgh: Clark, 1993.

Bauman, Richard. *For the Reputation of Truth: Politics, Religion, and Conflict among the Pennsylvania Quakers, 1750–1800*. Baltimore: Johns Hopkins University Press, 1971.

Bengel, Johann Albrecht. *Gnomon Novi Testamenti*. 1742.

Bittle, William G. James Nayler (1618–1660): *The Quaker Indicted by Parliament*. Richmond, IN: Friends United Press, 1986.

Blake, William. *A Vision of the Last Judgment*, in *Blake: Complete Writings*, edited by Geoffrey Keynes, 604–17. London: Oxford University Press, 1966.

Works Cited for the Entire Book

Borg, Marcus J., and John Dominic Crossan. *The First Christmas: What the Gospels Really Teach about Jesus's Birth*. New York: HarperCollins, 2007.

Boulton, David. "'Elves, Goblins, Fairies, Quakers, and New Lights': Friends in the English Republic." *Journal of the Friends Historical Society* 63 (2012), 3–19.

Brinton, Howard H. "Christianity and Conscription," *Pendle Hill Bulletin* #60. Wallingford, PA: Pendle Hill Publications, 1945.

———. "Moral Values and Mass Pressure," *Pendle Hill Bulletin* #82. Wallingford, PA: Pendle Hill Publications, 1948.

Brock, Peter. *The Quaker Peace Testimony, 1660–1914*. York, England: Sessions Books, 1990.

Brock, Peter, and Nigel Young. *Pacifism in the Twentieth Century*. Toronto: Toronto University Press, 1999.

Burrough, Edward. *A Measure of the Times*. London, 1657.

Calvert, Jane. *Quaker Constitutionalism and the Political Thought of John Dickinson*. Cambridge: Cambridge University Press, 2009.

Chayes, Sarah. *Thieves of State: Why Corruption Threatens Global Security*. New York: Norton, 2015.

Clough, Patricia T. "The Affective Turn: Political Economy, Biomedia, and Bodies." In *The Affect Theory Reader*, edited by Melissa Gregg and Gregory J. Seigworth, 206–25. Durham: Duke University Press, 2010.

Collins, Adela Yarbro. *The Combat Myth in the Book of Revelation*, Eugene, OR: Wipf and Stock, 2001.

———. *Crisis and Catharsis: The Power of the Apocalypse*. Philadelphia: Westminster, 1984.

Conser, Walter H., Jr., Ronald M. McCarthy, David J. Toscano, and Gene Sharp, eds. *Resistance, Politics, and the American Struggle for Independence, 1765–1775*. Boulder: Lynne Rienner, 1986.

Corbett, Jim. *Goatwalking*. New York: Viking, 1991.

———. *The Sanctuary Church*. Pendle Hill Pamphlet #270. Wallingford, PA: Pendle Hill Publications, 1986.

Corbett, Jim, and Ricardo Elford. *The Servant Church*. Pendle Hill Pamphlet #328. Wallingford, PA: Pendle Hill Publications, 1996.

Cornell, Andrew. *Oppose and Propose! Lessons from Movement for a New Society*. Oakland, CA: AK Press, 2011.

Dale, Jonathan. *Quaker Social Testimony in Personal and Corporate Life*. Pendle Hill Pamphlet #360. Wallingford, PA: Pendle Hill Publications, 2002.

Damrosch, Leo. *The Sorrows of the Quaker Jesus: James Nayler and the Puritan Crackdown on the Free Spirit*. Cambridge, MA: Harvard University Press, 1996.

Dandelion, Pink, Douglas Gwyn, Rachel Muers, Brian Phillips, and Richard E. Sturm. *Towards Tragedy/Reclaiming Hope: Literature, Theology and Sociology in Conversation*. Aldershot, Hampshire, England: Ashgate, 2004.

Debord, Guy. *Society of the Spectacle*. Detroit: Black & Red Press, 1970.

Edwards, Thomas. *Gangraena*. London, 1646.

Elliott, John H. *Conflict, Community, and Honor: 1 Peter in Social-Scientific Perspective*. Eugene, OR: Cascade, 2007.

Enns, Fernando, Scott Holland, and Ann K. Riggs, eds. *Seeking Cultures of Peace: A Peace Church Conversation*. Telford, PA: Cascadia, 2004.

Fager, Chuck. *Study War Some More (If You Want to Work for Peace.)*. Fayetteville, NC: Quaker House, 2010.

Fell, Margaret. *A Declaration and an Information from us the People of God called Quakers, to the Present Governors, the King and Both Houses of Parliament, and to all whom it may Concern*. London, 1660.

Fiorenza, Elisabeth Schüssler. *The Book of Revelation: Justice and Judgment*. 2nd ed. Minneapolis: Fortress, 1998.

———. *Invitation to the Book of Revelation: A Commentary on the Apocalypse with Complete Text from the Jerusalem Bible*. Garden City, NY: Image Books, 1981.

Fox, George. *Journal of George Fox*. Edited by Wilson Armistead. London: Friends Tract Association, 1891.

———. *The Journal of George Fox*. Edited by Norman Penney. Cambridge: Cambridge University Press, 1911.

———. *Journal of George Fox*. Edited by John L. Nickalls. Cambridge: Cambridge University Press, 1952.

———. *To the Councill of Officers of the Armie, and the Heads of the Nation, and for the Inferior Officers and Souldiers to read*. London, 1659.

———. *The Works of George Fox*. 8 vols. Philadelphia: Gould, 1831.

Fukuyama, Francis. *The End of History and the Last Man*. New York: Free Press, 2006.

Girard, René. *I See Satan Fall Like Lightning*. Maryknoll, NY: Orbis, 2001.

———. *Things Hidden since the Foundation of the World*. Stanford: Stanford University Press, 1986.

Gregg, Richard B. *The Power of Non-Violence*. Philadelphia: Lippincott, 1935.

Gross, Bertram. *Friendly Fascism: The New Face of Power in America*. Boston: South End Press, 1999.

Guiton, Gerard. *The Early Quakers and the 'Kingdom of God': Peace, Testimony and Revolution*. San Francisco: Inner Light Books, 2012.

Gwyn, Douglas. *Apocalypse of the Word: The Life and Message of George Fox*. Richmond, IN: Friends United Press, 1986.

———. *Conversation with Christ: Quaker Meditations on the Gospel of John.* Philadelphia: Quaker Press, 2011.

———. *The Covenant Crucified: Quakers and the Rise of Capitalism.* Wallingford, PA: Pendle Hill, 1995.

———. "The Early Quaker Lamb's War: Secularization and the Death of Tragedy in Early Modern England." In Pink Dandelion, Douglas Gwyn, Rachel Muers, Brian Phillips, and Richard E. Sturm, *Towards Tragedy/Reclaiming Hope: Literature, Theology and Sociology in Conversation,* 33–56. Aldershot, Hampshire, England: Ashgate, 2004.

———. "Enacting Truth: The Dynamics of Quaker Practice." *Quaker Theology* 17 (Spring–Summer 2010): 15–47.

———. "George Fox's Witness Regarding Good and Evil." In Jackie Leach Scully and Pink Dandelion, eds., *Good and Evil: Quaker Perspectives,* 31–42. Aldershot, Hampshire, England: Ashgate, 2007.

———. "James Nayler and the Lamb's War." *Quaker Studies* 12, no. 2 (2008): 171–88.

———. *Personality and Place: The Life and Times of Pendle Hill.* Philadelphia: Plain Press, 2014.

———. "Quakers, Eschatology, and Time." In *The Oxford Handbook of Quaker Studies,* edited by Stephen W. Angell and Pink Dandelion, 202–17. Oxford: Oxford University Press, 2013.

———. *Report from the Middle: Reflections on Divisions among Friends Today.* Boston: Beacon Hill Friends House, 2005.

———. *Seekers Found: Atonement in Early Quaker Experience.* Wallingford, PA: Pendle Hill Publications, 2000.

———. *A Sustainable Life: Quaker Faith and Practice in the Renewal of Creation.* Philadelphia: Quaker Press, 2014.

———. *Words in Time: Essays and Addresses.* Bellefont, PA: Kimo Press, 1997. http://quakertheology.org/GwynBook--RV-12-2015.pdf.

Hampton, Jenifer May. "British Quaker Survey: Examining Religious Beliefs and Practices in the Twenty-First Century." *Quaker Studies* 19, no. 1 (September 2014): 7–136.

Hardt, Michael, and Antonio Negri. *Empire.* Cambridge: Harvard University Press, 2000.

———. *Multitude: War and Democracy in the Age of Empire.* New York: Penguin, 2004.

Hill, Christopher. *The World Turned Upside Down: Radical Ideas during the English Revolution.* New York: Penguin, 1975.

Howgill, Francis. *The Works of Francis Howgill.* London, 1676.

Jameson, Fredric. *Postmodernism, or, the Cultural Logic of Late Capitalism.* Durham: Duke University Press, 1991.

Kahl, Brigitte. *Galatians Re-Imagined: Reading with the Eyes of the Vanquished.* Philadelphia: Fortress, 2010.

Käsemann, Ernst. *Commentary on Romans.* Grand Rapids, MI: Eerdmans, 1980.

Kuenning, Licia, ed. *Historical Writings of Quakers against War.* Glenside, PA: Quaker Heritage Press, 2002.

Marable, Manning. *How Capitalism Underdeveloped Black America.* Boston: South End Press, 2000.

Martyn, J. Louis. *Galatians.* Anchor Bible Commentary. New York: Doubleday, 1997.

Massumi, Brian. "The Future Birth of the Affective Fact: The Political Ontology of Threat." In *The Affect Theory Reader,* edited by Melissa Gregg and Gregory J. Seigworth, 52–70. Durham: Duke University Press, 2010.

Masters, Stuart. "Review." *Journal of the Friends Historical Society* 64 (2013): 22–25.

McClelland, Grigor. "The Prophet and the Reconciler." In *Endeavours to Mend: Perspectives on British Quaker Work in the World Today*, edited by Brian Phillips and John Lampen, 25–33. London: Quaker Books, 2006.

Meeks, Wayne A. *The First Urban Christians: The Social World of the Apostle Paul*. New Haven: Yale University Press, 1983.

Mekeel, Arthur J. *The Quakers and the American Revolution*. York, England: Sessions Book Trust, 1996.

Melman, Seymour. *The Permanent War Economy: American Capitalism in Decline*. New York: Simon & Schuster, 1976.

Moore, Rosemary. *The Light in Their Consciences: The Early Quakers in Britain, 1646–1666*. University Park: Pennsylvania State University Press, 2000.

Nayler, James. *The Works of James Nayler*. 4 vols. Glenside, PA: Quaker Heritage Press, 2003–2009.

Neelon, David. "James Nayler in the English Civil Wars." *Quaker Studies* 6 (2001): 8–36.

Nouwen, Henri. *Reaching Out: The Three Movements of the Spiritual Life*. New York: Image/Doubleday, 1975.

Palmer, Parker J. *The Company of Strangers: Christians and the Renewal of America's Public Life*. New York: Crossroad, 1981.

———. *Healing the Heart of Democracy: The Courage to Create a Politics Worthy of the Human Spirit*. San Francisco: Jossey-Bass, 2011.

Patterson, James T. *Grand Expectations: The United States, 1945–1971*. Oxford: Oxford University Press, 1996.

Penington, Isaac. *Right, Safety and Liberty*. London, 1651.

Punshon, John. *Reasons for Hope: The Faith and Future of the Friends Church*. Richmond, IN: Friends United Press, 2001.

Rodney, Walter. *How Europe Underdeveloped Africa*. Washington, DC: Howard University Press, 1974.

Rowland, Christopher C. "The Book of Revelation." In *The New Interpreter's Bible: Hebrews–Revelation*, vol. 12, 501–743. Nashville: Abingdon Press, 1998.

Salmon, Joseph. *A Rout, a Rout*. London, 1649.

Schmidt, Leigh Eric. *Restless Souls: The Making of American Spirituality*. San Francisco: Harper, 2005.

Smith, Nigel, ed. *A Collection of Ranter Writings from the 17th Century*. London: Junction Books, 1983.

Sommerville, Charles J. *The Secularisation of Early Modern England: From Religious Culture to Religious Faith*. Oxford: Oxford University Press, 1992.

Stringfellow, William. *Conscience and Obedience: The Politics of Romans 13 and Revelation 13 in Light of the Second Coming*. Waco, TX: Word Books, 1977.

Thrift, Nigel. "Understanding the Material Practices of Glamour." In *The Affect Theory Reader*, edited by Melissa Gregg and Gregory J. Seigworth, 289–308. Durham: Duke University Press, 2010.

von Rad, Gerhard. *Old Testament Theology*. 2 vols. New York: Harper, 1962.

Weddle, Meredith Baldwin. *Walking in the Way of Peace: Quaker Pacifism in the Seventeenth Century*. Oxford: Oxford University Press, 2001.

Wilken, Robert. *The Christians as the Romans Saw Them*. New Haven: Yale University Press, 1984.

Wink, Walter. *Engaging the Powers: Discernment and Resistance in a World of Domination*. Philadelphia: Fortress, 1992.

———. *The Human Being: Jesus and the Enigma of the Son of Man*. Minneapolis: Augsburg Books, 2001.

———. *Unmasking the Powers: The Invisible Forces That Determine Human Existence.* Philadelphia: Fortress, 1986.

Winstanley, Gerrard. *A Declaration of the Bloudie and Unchristian Acting.* 1649.

Woolman, John. *Journal and Major Essays.* Edited by Phillips P. Moulton. New York: Oxford University Press, 1971.

Young, Mildred Binns. *Another Will Gird You: A Message to the Society of Friends.* Pendle Hill Pamphlet #109. Wallingford, PA: Pendle Hill Publications, 1960.

[100] See Jane Calvert's provocative thesis on Quaker politics in her *Quaker Constitutionalism and the Political Thought of John Dickinson* (Cambridge: Cambridge University Press, 2009).

[101] Richard Gregg, *The Power of Non-Violence* (Philadelphia: Lippincott, 1935). For more on Gregg and his influence, see Gwyn, *Personality and Place*, 67–81.

[102] For more on Fox's proto-environmental ethic, see Gwyn, *A Sustainable Life*, introduction and chap. 8.

[103] For more on the peace testimony and its paradoxes, see Gwyn, *A Sustainable Life*, chap. 7.

[104] Gerhard von Rad, *Old Testament Theology* (New York: Harper, 1962), 1:130. For more on covenant and the early Quaker movement as a covenantal initiative at the dawn of capitalist society, see Gwyn, *The Covenant Crucified*.

[105] Marcus J. Borg and John Dominic Crossan, *The First Christmas: What the Gospels Really Teach about Jesus's Birth* (New York: HarperCollins, 2007), 69.

[106] For example, see the published reaction of Richard Baxter, parish minister at Leominster, in Gwyn, *Apocalypse of the Word*, 174–75.

[107] For more on the Quaker testimony of integrity and the spiritual practice of discernment that helps us grow into integrity, see Gwyn, *A Sustainable Life*, chap. 3.

[108] Chiasm, a term I used earlier in this essay, has its root in the Greek letter *chi*, or X.

Endnotes

[86] This was famously explored in Christopher Hill's *The World Turned Upside Down: Radical Ideas during the English Revolution* (New York: Penguin, 1975).

[87] George Fox, Epistle 51, in *The Works of George Fox*, 7:66.

[88] See Douglas Gwyn, *A Sustainable Life: Quaker Faith and Practice in the Renewal of Creation* (Philadelphia: Quaker Press, 2014) chap. 4, for further treatment of the interaction of equality and community.

[89] Fox, Epistle 227, in *The Works of George Fox*, 7:241.

[90] See Gwyn, *Seekers Found*, 407–8.

[91] For revealing interviews on the history of the Movement for a New Society, see Andrew Cornell, *Oppose and Propose! Lessons from Movement for a New Society* (Oakland, CA: AK Press, 2011).

[92] Parker J. Palmer, *The Company of Strangers: Christians and the Renewal of America's Public Life* (New York: Crossroad, 1981); Parker J. Palmer, *Healing the Heart of Democracy: The Courage to Create a Politics Worthy of the Human Spirit* (San Francisco: Jossey-Bass, 2011).

[93] In a similar vein, during the American Revolution some American Friends, such as the minister Job Scott, refused to use either English or colonial money because both were used to finance the war.

[94] Fox, *Journal*, ed. Nickalls, 27.

[95] For more on the Quaker testimony of simplicity within the horizon of a vision for sustainability, see Gwyn, *A Sustainable Life*, chap. 8.

[96] John Woolman, *Journal and Major Essays*, ed. Phillips P. Moulton (New York: Oxford University Press, 1971), 239–40.

[97] Nayler, *The Works of James Nayler* (Glenside, PA: Quaker Heritage Press, 2004), 2:584–85.

[98] Jonathan Dale, *Quaker Social Testimony in Personal and Corporate Life*, Pendle Hill Pamphlet #360 (Wallingford, PA: Pendle Hill Publications, 2002), 28.

[99] See Walter Wink, *Engaging the Powers: Discernment and Resistance in a World of Domination* (Philadelphia: Fortress, 1992), 175–84.

74 Sarah Chayes, *Thieves of State: Why Corruption Threatens Global Security* (New York: Norton, 2015).

75 The first English translation was published in 1970 by Black & Red Press. Also see Hardt and Negri, *Empire*, 188, 321–23.

76 For a useful analysis, see Nigel Thrift, "Understanding the Material Practices of Glamour," in *The Affect Theory Reader*, ed. Melissa Gregg and Gregory J. Seigworth (Durham: Duke University Press, 2010), 289–308.

77 So where is the greater "terror"? Since 2001, approximately 3,100 Americans have been killed through terrorist acts, of which all but about 100 occurred on September 11, 2001. Over the same period, more than 400,000 Americans have died from gunshot wounds.

78 For more on this theme, see Francis Fukuyama, *The End of History and the Last Man* (New York: Free Press, 2006), chap. 28.

79 Brian Massumi, "The Future Birth of the Affective Fact: The Political Ontology of Threat," in Gregg and Seigworth, *The Affect Theory Reader*, 52–70.

80 For a critique of this tendency by the historic peace churches, see "Just Peacemaking: Toward an Ecumenical Ethical Approach from the Perspective of the Historic Peace Churches," in Fernando Enns, Scott Holland, and Ann K. Riggs, eds., *Seeking Cultures of Peace: A Peace Church Conversation* (Telford, PA: Cascadia, 2004), 238–40.

81 Bertram Gross, *Friendly Fascism: The New Face of Power in America* (Boston: South End Press, 1999).

82 Henri Nouwen, *Reaching Out: The Three Movements of the Spiritual Life* (New York: Image/Doubleday, 1975), 118.

83 Michelle Alexander, *The New Jim Crow: Mass Incarceration in the Age of Color Blindness* (New York: New Press, 2012).

84 Walter Rodney, *How Europe Underdeveloped Africa* (1973), 216, as quoted in Manning Marable, *How Capitalism Underdeveloped Black America* (Boston: South End Press, 2000), 231.

85 See Patricia T. Clough, "The Affective Turn: Political Economy, Biomedia, and Bodies," in *The Affect Theory Reader*, 206–25.

Endnotes

[61] Howard H. Brinton, *Moral Values and Mass Pressure*, Pendle Hill Bulletin #82 (Wallingford, PA: Pendle Hill Publications, 1948).

[62] Ibid.

[63] Seymour Melman, *The Permanent War Economy: American Capitalism in Decline* (New York: Simon & Schuster, 1976).

[64] An excellent treatment of these economic and military interactions can be found in Giovanni Arrighi, *The Long Twentieth Century: Money, Power and the Origins of Our Times* (New York: Verso, 1994).

[65] As quoted in James T. Patterson, *Grand Expectations: The United States, 1945–1971* (Oxford: Oxford University Press, 1996), 69.

[66] As quoted in Chuck Fager, *Study War Some More (If You Want to Work for Peace.)* (Fayetteville, NC: Quaker House, 2010), 14.

[67] The speech was drafted for King by his friend and associate in the Civil Rights Movement Vincent Harding, who had various Quaker connections and taught at Pendle Hill from 1979 to 1981, returning briefly in 2013 just before his death. See Douglas Gwyn, *Personality and Place: The Life and Times of Pendle Hill* (Philadelphia: Plain Press, 2014), 297.

[68] Again, see Arrighi, *The Long Twentieth Century*, for an analysis of these different configurations, down to the United States-centered global economy.

[69] Michael Hardt and Antonio Negri, *Empire* (Cambridge: Harvard University Press, 2000).

[70] Fredric Jameson, *Postmodernism, or, the Cultural Logic of Late Capitalism* (Durham: Duke University Press, 1991).

[71] For a fuller treatment of Fox on the subject of evil, see Douglas Gwyn, "George Fox's Witness Regarding Good and Evil," in Jackie Leach Scully and Pink Dandelion, eds., *Good and Evil: Quaker Perspectives* (Aldershot, Hampshire, England: Ashgate, 2007), 31–42.

[72] Hardt and Negri, *Empire*, 189; also see their *Multitude: War and Democracy in the Age of Empire* (New York: Penguin, 2004), chap. 1.1.

[73] See Hardt and Negri, *Empire*, 201–2.

54 James Nayler, *The Lamb's War*, in Hugh Barbour and Arthur Roberts, eds., *Early Quaker Writings, 1650–1700* (Grand Rapids: Eerdmans, 1973), 106.

55 Ibid., 111, 114.

56 My interpretation here differs from that of Leo Damrosch in *The Sorrows of the Quaker Jesus: James Nayler and the Puritan Crackdown on the Free Spirit* (Cambridge, MA: Harvard University Press, 1996), 62–68.

57 Nayler, *The Works of James Nayler*, 4:406–8.

58 I explore the resonances between tragedy and apocalyptic theology in Douglas Gwyn, "The Early Quaker Lamb's War: Secularization and the Death of Tragedy in Early Modern England," in Pink Dandelion et al., *Towards Tragedy/Reclaiming Hope: Literature, Theology and Sociology in Conversation* (Aldershot, Hampshire, England: Ashgate, 2004), 33–56.

59 For an extensive study of the nonviolent resistance to British imperial control up to 1775, see Walter H. Conser Jr., Ronald M. McCarthy, David J. Toscano, and Gene Sharp, eds., *Resistance, Politics, and the American Struggle for Independence, 1765–1775* (Boulder: Lynne Rienner, 1986). Nonviolent forms of resistance included boycotts, non-importation, non-cooperation, and various protest demonstrations. The book counters prevailing histories of the American Revolution that treat these nonviolent resistances merely as prelude to the inevitable progress toward war. Spencer Graves argues that colonial innovations augured for a more democratic society than what resulted from the violent American Revolution. Spencer Graves, "Violence, Nonviolence, and the American Revolution," *Productive Systems Engineering*, http://www.prodsyse.com/. Or, as Quaker nonviolent action theorist George Lakey writes, "The more violence, the less revolution." George Lakey, "The More Violence, the Less Revolution," *Waging Nonviolence*, March 6, 2012, http://wagingnonviolence.org/feature/the-more-violence-the-less-revolution/. For a revealing study of Quaker efforts on both sides of the Atlantic to mediate the growing conflict between Britain and its American colonies, see Arthur J. Mekeel, *The Quakers and the American Revolution* (York, England: Sessions Book Trust, 1996).

60 Howard H. Brinton, *Christianity and Conscription*, Pendle Hill Bulletin #60 (Wallingford, PA: Pendle Hill Publications, 1945).

Reformers are better known to us today through their modern-day descendants, the Mennonites, Amish, and Hutterites. Their indirect influence on the pre-Quaker milieu in England is addressed in chapter 3 of *Seekers Found*.

[38] George Fox, *The Lamb's Officer* (1659), in *The Works of George Fox*, 4:187.

[39] George Fox, Epistle 222 (1662), in *The Works of George Fox*, 7:234.

[40] Fox, *Journal of George Fox*, ed. Wilson Armistead (London: Friends Tract Association 1891), 1:420.

[41] Fox, *The Works of George Fox*, 2:192.

[42] Fox, *The cause why Adam and Eve were driven out of Paradise* (1682), in *The Works of George Fox*, 6:158.

[43] Francis Howgill, *The Works of Francis Howgill* (London, 1676), 210.

[44] Fox, *Journal*, ed. Nickalls, 22.

[45] Fox, *The Works of George Fox*, 3:99.

[46] Fox, "Epistle to the King of Austria" (1660), in *The Works of George Fox*, 4:229.

[47] For a larger account of the scope and revolutionary aims of the Lamb's War, see the early chapters of Gwyn, *The Covenant Crucified*.

[48] Fox, *The Works of George Fox*, 4:18–19.

[49] Nayler, *The Works of James Nayler*, 1:185–86.

[50] Ibid., 1:196–97, 203–4.

[51] Nayler, *The Works of James Nayler*, 2:583.

[52] Ibid., 584–85.

[53] As quoted in William G. Bittle, *James Nayler (1618–1660): The Quaker Indicted by Parliament* (Richmond, IN: Friends United Press, 1986), 106.

Experience (Wallingford, PA: Pendle Hill Publications, 2000), 174–75. For the full Salmon text, see Nigel Smith, ed., *A Collection of Ranter Writings from the 17th Century* (London: Junction Books, 1983), 190ff.

[28] As quoted in Gwyn, *Seekers Found*, 176.

[29] Gerrard Winstanley, *A Declaration of the Bloudie and Unchristian Acting* (1649), 4-5, as quoted in Gwyn, *Seekers Found*, 146.

[30] For this treatment of Nayler, I mainly draw from my earlier work, Douglas Gwyn, "James Nayler and the Lamb's War," *Quaker Studies* 12, no.2 (2008): 171–88. For Nayler in the larger context of the Lamb's War, see Douglas Gwyn, *The Covenant Crucified: Quakers and the Rise of Capitalism* (Wallingford, PA: Pendle Hill, 1995; reprinted London: Quaker Books, 2006), particularly chap. 5.

[31] David Neelon has researched Nayler's military service more fully than anyone before. See David Neelon, "James Nayler in the English Civil Wars," *Quaker Studies* 6 (2001), 8–36.

[32] James Nayler, *The Works of James Nayler*, 1:33–34.

[33] Nayler, *The Works of James Nayler*, 4:78–79.

[34] George Fox, *Journal of George Fox,* ed. John L. Nickalls (Cambridge: Cambridge University Press, 1952), 8.

[35] George Fox, *The Works of George Fox* (Philadelphia: Gould, 1831), 5:127–41. That tract, however, was not written until 1677, and Fox's interpretation of Revelation had shifted somewhat to engage with the long-term future of the movement in relation to a restored monarchy and national church. His earlier use of Revelation has to be pieced together from that tract plus briefer uses of Revelation during the early, revolutionary phase of the movement.

[36] An earlier review of Fox's thought in this regard can be found in Douglas Gwyn, *Apocalypse of the Word: The Life and Message of George Fox* (Richmond, IN: Friends United Press, 1986; 2nd ed. 2014), chap. 11.

[37] Spiritualist reformers formed the far-left wing of the Protestant Reformation, with their emphasis upon the spiritual presence of Christ within as primary authority. I give more attention to these important Quaker precursors, particularly Caspar Schwenckfeld and Sebastian Franck, in chapter 2 of *Seekers Found*. The Anabaptist

might have thought about more mutual, loving homosexual relations—if he even knew of such things.

16 See Walter Wink, *Unmasking the Powers: The Invisible Forces That Determine Human Existence* (Philadelphia: Fortress, 1986).

17 See Elisabeth Schüssler Fiorenza, *Invitation to the Book of Revelation: A Commentary on the Apocalypse with Complete Text from the Jerusalem Bible* (Garden City, NY: Image Books, 1981), 84.

18 Adela Yarbro Collins, *The Combat Myth in the Book of Revelation* (Eugene, OR: Wipf and Stock, 2001). This is a publication of her groundbreaking 1975 Harvard PhD dissertation.

19 The work of René Girard and his followers has made this meaning of the cross more explicit to modern understanding. For an introduction to Girard's work, see René Girard, *I See Satan Fall Like Lightning* (Maryknoll, NY: Orbis, 2001). For a fuller account of his thesis, see René Girard, *Things Hidden since the Foundation of the World* (Stanford: Stanford University Press, 1987).

20 Fiorenza, *Invitation to the Book of Revelation*, 135.

21 See Collins, *The Combat Myth*, 126.

22 Regarding Babylon, I have been particularly helped by Richard Bauckham, *The Climax of Prophecy: Studies on the Book of Revelation* (Edinburgh: Clark, 1993), chap. 9 ("The Economic Critique of Rome in Revelation 18").

23 See Fiorenza, *The Book of Revelation: Justice and Judgment*, epilogue.

24 Brigitte Kahl offers an extended interpretation of the Pergamum altar, relating it to Paul's letter to the Galatians (Christian Gauls/Celts in Asia Minor), in Brigitte Kahl, *Galatians Re-Imagined: Reading with the Eyes of the Vanquished* (Philadelphia: Fortress, 2010).

25 Walter Wink, *The Human Being: Jesus and the Enigma of the Son of Man* (Minneapolis: Augsburg Books, 2001), 152.

26 Alain Badiou, *Saint Paul: The Foundation of Universalism* (Palo Alto: Stanford University Press, 2003).

27 From Joseph Salmon, *A Rout, a Rout* (London, 1649), as quoted in Douglas Gwyn, *Seekers Found: Atonement in Early Quaker*

The New Interpreter's Bible: Hebrews–Revelation, vol. 12 (Nashville: Abingdon, 1998), 542.

7 William Blake, *A Vision of the Last Judgment,* in *Blake: Complete Writings*, ed. Geoffrey Keynes (London: Oxford University Press, 1966), 617, as quoted in Rowland, "The Book of Revelation," 507.

8 For a Quaker reading of the Gospel of John, see Douglas Gwyn, *Conversation with Christ: Quaker Meditations on the Gospel of John* (Philadelphia: Quaker Press, 2011).

9 Adela Yarbro Collins, *Crisis and Catharsis: The Power of the Apocalypse* (Philadelphia: Westminster, 1984), chap. 1.

10 Pliny's procedure with Christians while governor of Asia Minor is quoted in Fiorenza, *The Book of Revelation: Justice and Judgment*, 193. For more on Pliny and the early Christians, see Robert Wilken, *The Christians as the Romans Saw Them* (New Haven: Yale University Press, 1984), chap. 1.

11 For a much fuller treatment of John's opponents among the churches of Asia Minor, see Fiorenza, *The Book of Revelation: Justice and Judgment,* chap. 4.

12 William Stringfellow addresses the contrast between Paul and John in his *Conscience and Obedience: The Politics of Romans 13 and Revelation 13 in Light of the Second Coming* (Waco, TX: Word Books, 1977).

13 The wrath of God as the final restoration of divine justice against human immorality, violence, and injustice grows throughout the Hebrew prophetic literature, from Amos 5:18–20 and Isaiah 2:5–22 to the apocalyptic literature, exemplified by Daniel's prayer for mercy toward Israel in Daniel 9:3–19 and intertestamental literature such as Enoch and the Dead Sea Scrolls.

14 The apocalyptic interpretation of Paul's thought can be found laid out most fully in works such as Ernst Käsemann, *Commentary on Romans* (Grand Rapids, MI: Eerdmans, 1980) and J. Louis Martyn, *Galatians*, Anchor Bible Commentary (New York: Doubleday, 1997).

15 We can simply let Paul be a man of his times on the matter of homosexuality. But it's worth noting that some modern scholars suggest that Paul, who had not yet been to Rome at the time of his writing this, was probably thinking here of the unequal and exploitative homosexual relationships with slaves and with youth for which the imperial city was notorious. We don't know what Paul

NOTES

[1] See the full quotation in Nayler, *The Works of James Nayler* (Glenside, PA: Quaker Heritage Press, 2009), 4:382. These are often cited as Nayler's dying words (he was badly beaten by unknown attackers and died of the injuries in 1660), but they had appeared in a publication of various short pieces by Nayler a year before his death.

[2] Chiasm is a literary device, a sequence of ideas or themes that then repeats itself in reverse order. Chiastic structuring is found in Revelation and many other parts of the Bible. It is also found in ancient Greek literature. On a practical level, chiasm may have been a mnemonic device, subliminally aiding in the retention of a story or discourse in an age when texts were often heard read aloud. But on a deeper level, chiasm hints at a deeper meaning revealed in the structure of the text itself, not just its content.

[3] John Punshon reviews various millennialisms imported by evangelical Friends in the nineteenth century from the wider evangelical movement. He concludes correctly that early Friends, like Augustine, were *amillennial* in their outlook; they ignored Revelation 20:4 and its tendency to inspire speculative prediction. See John Punshon, *Reasons for Hope: The Faith and Future of the Friends Church* (Richmond, IN: Friends United Press, 2001), chap. 9.

[4] Eschatology refers to beliefs in last things (the Greek *eschatos* means "end" or "last"), ranging from personal death to the end of the world. Eschatology almost always interacts in one way or another with teleology, that other sense of "end" (the Greek *telos* means "end" as "purpose" or "aim"). Christian eschatology searches for some meaningful end, some fulfillment of God's purposes in history, in the creation of the universe. For a review of various Quaker eschatologies and teleologies, see Douglas Gwyn, "Quakers, Eschatology, and Time," in *The Oxford Handbook of Quaker Studies*, ed. Stephen W. Angell and Pink Dandelion (Oxford: Oxford University Press, 2013), 202–17.

[5] Elisabeth Schüssler Fiorenza, *The Book of Revelation: Justice and Judgment*, 2nd ed. (Minneapolis: Fortress, 1998), 46.

[6] Johann Albrecht Bengel, *Gnomon Novi Testamenti* (1742), 1026, as quoted in Christopher C. Rowland, "The Book of Revelation," in

articulate a lived sense of that structural reality. We have seen how this covenant engages and subverts the violent power of the Dragon—a power the Dragon possesses only so far as the inhabitants of the earth cede it, through delusion, desire, and fear.

I first posed the rubric of "X-Covenant" over twenty years ago, in the conclusion to *The Covenant Crucified: Quakers and the Rise of Capitalism*. That book explored the covenantal dynamics of the early Quaker movement as a nonviolent cultural revolution with an apocalyptic theology. The conclusion was a first attempt at bringing those insights from early Friends to bear on the current challenges of global capitalism. I used the X to denote a way of exploring covenantal community as *ex*odus from the captivity of the capitalist regime and to mark an open, indeterminate space where Christian and universalist, theist and nontheist, activist and contemplative resisters of the system meet in convergent revolutionary practice.

This essay has developed the concept of the X-Covenant more fully as the structure of revolutionary practice, which also reveals the true nature of the Dragon and its forces. Meanwhile, this essay is wedded to the other essay in this book in a chiastic structure.[108] The two essays of this book thus exist in a continuous process of dialectical overturnings, which I hope will generate new insights for readers as it has for me in the process of writing. Therefore, "Maranatha! Come Lord Jesus!" (Revelation 22:20) at every turn of the process, each of which is the End.

Conclusion: The One, the Alpha and the Omega, the X-Covenant

John's visions begin as he is "in the Spirit on the Lord's day" on the island of Patmos (Revelation 1:10). He is taken up in the Spirit to heaven, "and there in heaven stood a throne, with one seated on the throne" (4:2). All of John's revelations in their complex structure radiate from that throne where this One is seated. The throne is an image of divine authority and will. It is the center of coherence, the only center that holds against the violence and destructive lust of the Dragon. Hence, the One abides at the center of Figure 2. There is no question that John means that "one" to be God, the Lord of Israel, the creator and destiny of all that is. "I am the Alpha and the Omega, says the Lord God, who is and who was and who is to come, the Almighty" (1:8). Although Revelation does retain some linear sense of future end-time expectation, this essay has suggested that the End is everywhere in the book's structure. But it abides pre-eminently at the center, from which everything radiates and returns.

John opts to describe the presence on the throne as "one" rather than "God," which after all is a generic term. The One is not generic but generative. It is the place of unknowing at the center of our being, the place where we continually return, to be led back out in patterns of covenantal faithfulness. The light of the throne and the Lamb illuminates the entire city of new Jerusalem. The One generates the structure explored in this essay. The four corners of the chart in Figure 2 form an X. As we have seen in this essay, each corner constitutes a particular aspect of the covenantal reality of a peculiar people whose peace finds God's purposes in history. We have found that the Quaker testimonies and Jesus' teaching in the Sermon on the Mount

93

ultimate purposes are not known to us. We can only strive to remain faithful in speaking truth to power, remaining close to our source, the light of Christ in our hearts. Militarism is the justification of violent means to achieve ends that never seem to work out as nobly as they were stated. The anti-war is the militant inversion of militarism; it is faithfulness in peaceful means toward ends yet to be revealed, leaving all justifications to God alone. The covenant is a space defined by *shalom*, a space where we converge and attempt to remain. It has no particular purpose but to glorify God, whose patterns and purposes are "too wonderful for me" (Job 42:3). (See the essay on the other side of this book for converse reflections on the right and left hands of God.)

Readers may be disappointed that this section's treatment of the Quaker testimonies features little in the way of concrete examples or prescriptions. There are many initiatives and experiments among Friends today in North America, Britain, East Africa, Latin America, and elsewhere, ranging from heroic, prophetic confrontations with social injustice and militarism to more quiet and integrative work to exert the centripetal power of God in society and the environment. But these are perhaps too situation-specific and time-bound to be helpful in this book. The purpose here is to portray the overall structural dynamics of the anti-war, with the hope that a vision of the whole may help inspire renewed discernment and action among Friends in specific times and places.

The testimonies and other elements of Quaker faith and practice that have been integrated into this map of the anti-war may also be found in my recent book, *A Sustainable Life: Quaker Faith and Practice in the Renewal of Creation* (2014). That book reframes traditional aspects of Quaker faith and practice in terms of an integrative sustainability on personal, social, and environmental levels. The same elements are refocused here in terms of our conflict with the dominant powers of our age.

The Anti-War

Likewise, early Friends didn't seek to overthrow the government or redistribute wealth in England; rather, they attacked the religious establishment that sanctified unjust power and economic exploitation. Our conflict is the same, in the circumstances of our time. Our faithful life of covenant testimony counters the system at all four corners, as this essay shows. But by engaging this last corner of the structure we shake the foundations of the entire structure.

The middle, mediating terms at this corner of Figure 2 are *ideology* and *theory*. As with all the other mediating elements, these are ambiguous and can be pulled either inward, toward the centripetal, binding force of covenant, or toward the centrifugal, entropic forces of death and destruction. Modern liberal Quakerism has been strongly aligned with the ideology of the liberal Enlightenment, which converges with Quaker faith and practices in a variety of ways. But liberal Friends have often substituted that ideology for the true, liberating power of the gospel in traditional Quaker understanding. That confusion has compromised the militancy of our tradition and helped shape our comfortable, middle-class profile.

My own work in Quaker history and theology has utilized Marxist and other traditions of social *theory* as a corrective to that liberal ideologization of Quaker faith and practice, and as a lens to expose the capitalist ideology that lurks below the surface of liberalism. But I have sought to avoid a Marxist *ideology*, which proved so disastrous in the twentieth century. It is crucial—in the true sense of crucifying our hearts and minds to the world—that we discern carefully, at every step, the true gospel faith of our Quaker tradition from whatever ideological and theoretical thought frames that appear convergent with it.

The Word of God speaks through us, beyond our understandings, be they theological, theoretical, or ideological. That means, among other things, that God's

91

Confrontation with the False Prophet brings the Quaker testimony of *truth/integrity* most into focus.[107] Integrity means becoming the same in words as in life. It is integration of the different parts of our lives into one whole. It is only from that place that we can truly "speak truth to power," speak the prophetic word so urgently needed today. In the Sermon on the Mount, Jesus calls his disciples to "be perfect as your heavenly Father is perfect" (Matthew 5:48). The Greek word translated as "perfect" is *teleios*, which means perfect in the sense of maturity, wholeness, completeness, oneness. We are meant to be one as God is one, both individually and as a peculiar people of God. From that place, the militant Word of God, Faithful and True, speaks through us. Jesus said that "the eye is the lamp of the body. So if your eye is healthy [literally, "single"], your body will be full of light" (6:22). Integrity is the singleness of vision and coherence of life that not only brings us inner peace but makes us peacemakers in society.

But again, the covenant of peace also brings division. Jesus said,

> *I came to bring fire to the earth, and how I wish it were already kindled! I have a baptism with which to be baptized and what stress I am under until it is completed! Do you think I have come to bring peace to the earth? No, I tell you, but rather division! From now on five in one household will be divided, three against two and two against three.* (Luke 12:49–52)

Jesus initiated his conflict not with the Romans or the Jewish aristocracy and large landowners who oppressed his people but with the temple priesthood, scribes, and Pharisees who helped legitimate that regime. Similarly, John set out the four terms of the Dragon's reign in the Roman Empire, but the conflict was joined primarily through resistance to the blasphemous claims of the False Prophet, which mystified the reign of Babylon and the Beast. That is spiritual warfare.

both religious and secular—for the military-industrial complex. The term "fascist" is not a rhetorical flourish but a reasonable description of this phenomenon. Of course, there are many sincere, self-sacrificing ministers who offer unquestioning support and divine sanction to America's military-industrial complex. But, as in seventeenth-century England, the place they occupy and the role they fulfill in the overall structure of the Dragon's rule manifests their collective identity as False Prophet. As was the case in Nazi Germany and Fascist Italy, clergy face great pressure to add their ideological support to the regime. In America today, that pressure is not coercive. It often arises from within the congregation. But just as we rue the clergy who submitted to the intimidation of the Third Reich, so those who wrap themselves in the flag today will be exposed by the Word of God.

Of course, the secular ideologues of the Right are often even more pernicious. But their arrogant rhetorical brandishings are sheer ideology. When the churches submit gospel theology to such ideology, they crucify anew the Prince of Peace who was crucified by the Romans. The Word of God leads us into spiritual warfare with false prophets, both secular and religious.

Certainly, the decline in membership and attendance, even among conservative churches today, is mainly due to the ongoing secularization of American society and the consumerist individualism that numbs the human conscience. A few still find their way to a Friends meeting or another church that takes a stand for peace and justice against the military-industrial complex. But a more open confrontation with the military-industrial complex might produce a larger groundswell, just as the early Quaker movement drew so many of the most earnest young seekers through its relentless confrontation with the Dragon's forces of their time. This may sound like wishful thinking. But there was nothing in the situation of northern England in 1652 that made the Quaker outbreak there predictable.

There are many kinds of coalition between organizations in a pluralistic society. Not all take place under a thoroughgoing commitment to peace, but they are generally undertaken in peaceful ways that contribute to the health of civil society. Friends and other peacemaking groups will find themselves united in common cause for economic justice, human rights, or environmental concerns with various others whose concern for self-protection prevents them from the covenantal *shalom* we find incumbent upon us. This is a matter for case-by-case discernment. Coalition with some groups may lack integrity, owing to their violent philosophy, skewed sense of justice, or covert aims.

The Word of God: Purpose

In Revelation 19, Christ appears as a horseman called Faithful and True, the Word of God, followed by armies of heaven. "From his mouth comes a sharp sword" (19:11–15). Early Friends understood this imagery to suggest their spiritual battle for hearts and minds under the rubric of the Lamb's War. Their unprecedented campaign of tract warfare and systematic interruption of parish services was aimed most of all against the enfranchised clergy of the state-sponsored church, whom they understood to be the False Prophet of their time. Of course, many parish priests were genuine ministers, men sincere in their efforts to serve God and the members of their parish. Many no doubt felt unjustly maligned by these Quaker firebrands barging into their worship.[106] But the Quaker attack on the position of tithe-supported priests within the overall social structure and the class interests they inevitably served spoke compellingly to many Christians longing for the church to serve as catalyst to a more equitable society.

As suggested earlier, the False Prophet of our time is embodied by the right-wing ideologues and apologists—

defines a wholeness, a communion, a harmonious equilibrium that balances the needs and claims among parties—an intactness, orderliness, rightness.[104] Or, as New Testament scholars Marcus Borg and John Dominic Crossan summarize, empire's peace comes through victory; the kingdom (or covenant) of God brings peace with justice.[105]

Early Friends failed in their attempts to disestablish the church-state complex. They suffered massive persecutions; more than 12,000 were imprisoned and over 450 Friends died in their nonviolent Lamb's War offensive in England and Wales. But as "peace finds the purpose of a peculiar people," their faithfulness served divine purposes in certain ways they could not have anticipated. Their stubborn resistance finally helped achieve the Act of Toleration for nonconforming religious groups in England in 1689. It also contributed to the growth of multi-party politics, as their nonviolent suffering under persecution proved that opposition politics can be loyal to government even while maintaining a robust resistance. Moreover, Quaker influence in colonial America helped establish the pluralistic religious environment we cherish today. These contributions fall far short of the covenantal society early Friends hoped to establish. But they are constitutional advances that have surely served divine providence in history.

Today, Friends link with a wide variety of peace and justice-oriented groups to oppose the military-industrial complex on different fronts: protesting the new drone warfare and the use of torture and working for a more just criminal justice system, for the reform of prisons, and for gun control, to name just a few. These are all aims worthy in their own right. But they may also contribute to divine purposes that will become more evident only in hindsight.

The middle term in Figure 2 between peace/nonviolent action and the military-industrial complex is *coalition*.

Early Friends developed their sense of testimony in relation to their covenantal sense of the light. Their collective faith and practice was their testimony to the covenant they were enacting together. It defined a social space in the wider society, a space that *bound* them together in faithfulness and *separated* them from unjust and violent social norms and government policies. We have already explored that space in preceding sections in terms of Revelation's Mount Zion and new Jerusalem, terms that early Friends often used in writing about the Lamb's War.[103]

In the *peace testimony*, the anti-war inverts what counts for security in the military-industrial complex. True peace, not peace through domination and violence, is counterintuitive. As we gather into the light of God's presence, there is a sublime sense of stillness, peace, surrender, and communion with the divine. But as that space begins to take shape within and among us, we simultaneously see more clearly those aspects of our personal and social lives that are not peaceful, moral, or just. Paradoxically, to consolidate the peace, we must enter into conflict. We find ourselves led to confront and eliminate the parts of our lives that do not participate in the covenant, that do not make for peace. We enter this nonviolent struggle first of all in our personal lives, putting our own houses in order. But the conflict soon spreads to our interpersonal social and political lives. It sometimes leads to uncomfortable confrontations, risks to our employment or other sources of financial security. True peace doesn't make for what most people count as security, but it teaches us to know where true security is: "in the presence of God and these friends" (as the traditional Quaker wedding-covenant promise begins).

According to biblical scholar Gerhard von Rad, Hebrew Scripture most typically defines the quality of covenantal relationship with the word *shalom*, which we usually translate as "peace." But *shalom* connotes the reconciliation of various elements of existence. It

The Hebrew word for covenant, *berith*, means "to bind." The preceding descriptions of covenant emphasize its indeterminate reach, creating bonds of faithful relationship in all directions. But the Hebrew verb most often used to describe making a covenant is *karath*, "to cut." The bonds of friendship and love, identity, and shared action also necessarily draw lines that define what we *cannot* embrace. Just as the early Quaker covenant of light advanced a Lamb's War pre-eminently against the state-church complex of its day, so today's anti-war sets itself pre-eminently in opposition to the military-industrial complex. The latter is not only violent, exploitative, and polluting in epic proportions; it is also the most spiritually deforming force affecting human consciousness today—all the more so because we barely notice how powerful and pervasive its influence is.

Testimony, or *witness*, also derives from covenantal thought. Testimony is witness to the truth in words and actions, less in the propositional sense of true statements than in the participational sense of being true to what is real, right, and good. In the "Old Testament," after the Israelites enter the promised land, Joshua renews with them the covenant with the Lord (Yahweh), saying "you are witnesses" (*adim*, Joshua 24:22). They will *witness to the Lord* and the covenant as they pursue justice, which is their true security. Conversely, they will *witness against themselves* as they forsake the Lord for other gods and other definitions of security. In the succeeding history of ancient Israel, the prophets give testimony (e.g., Isaiah 8:16) in the Lord's covenant lawsuit against Israel and Judah, an indictment of their exploitation of the poor in the pursuit of military security, religious pomp, and royal majesty. In the "New Testament," the gospel message is testimony/witness (the Greek is *martyria*) in words, actions, and suffering to Jesus as the renewal and expansion of Israel's covenant.

faithfulness in our role as stewards of the creation. Love toward God's creatures knows no limit as we continue to grow into it.

By contrast, the military-industrial complex, today's embodiment of Babylon riding the Beast, is a devil's bargain, the "mother of harlots and earth's abominations" (17:5). It is the most potent defiler of human conscience, corrupting U.S. government and industry, science and technology. Internationally, it peddles weapons of death and destruction among the nations. It links international trade partnerships with U.S. military protection. Partner nations even find themselves open to legal attack by American-based corporations when they pursue policies to help their poor or conserve natural resources.

Meanwhile, domestically, the military-industrial complex casts long shadows on the American collective psyche. As noted earlier, police are becoming increasingly militarized in weaponry and tactics. Prisons brutally debase millions and act out the unexamined racism of American society. The National Rifle Association promotes gun fetishism and plays to the paranoid fantasies of white Americans fearful of African Americans on the one side and the federal government on the other. Military and police dramas saturate television and film and dominate video games. In spectator sports athletes become "weapons" against the other team. Conversely, enemy combatants on real battlefields are cast in banal, television terms as "bad guys." In all these ways and more, the American psyche is inured to the dictates of the military-industrial complex. As noted earlier, *security* becomes a watchword on all fronts: maximum-security prisons to protect us from the "bad guys" at home; overwhelming military security and invasive intelligence to protect us from the "bad guys" abroad; ever more destructive methods of coal, oil, and gas extraction to provide energy security and to protect us from the "bad guys" in the OPEC nations.

construe its guidance within whatever religious and cultural frameworks are available and most meaningful to them. Hence, the light cannot be definitively attached to formulations of doctrine. Beliefs are important but must remain grounded in personal and collective *experience* of the light's guidance. The light is also indeterminate in the sense that it is God's abiding presence, which is unconditional and always available. And when humans turn to the light and learn to abide there, a relationship of unbounded scope and possibility unfolds.

Second, the light is *indeterminate toward humanity*; it is impossible to judge the spiritual lives of other people. Others may be informed by the light in ways that simply do not fit our religious and moral conceptions. That doesn't mean that "anything goes" but that we must approach our differences with discernment rather than simplistic codes. The possibilities for covenantal friendship and shared action across religious differences are indeterminate. Again, friendship is a polymorphous idiom of relationship that enables a wide range of affinities and collaborations among humans. To be sure, religious communities and their traditions remain vital. Their particular idioms of faith and practice are the richest form of covenantal life. But they must resist the temptation to become self-referential and self-justifying. There are endless ways in which communities can interconnect through networks of concerted faithful action. Covenant is where we find it.

Finally, the light is *indeterminate toward the creation.* Because the light abides within us below the level of human language, it fosters our compassion toward the rest of God's creatures. (The Woolman quotation in the preceding section offers testimony to that reality.) George Fox taught that the light gives insight into the wisdom of God that created all things and will lead us into right relationship and balanced use of God's creatures. Without that wisdom, humans "devour the creation."[102] The light engenders a sense of covenantal through his book *The Power of Non-Violence*. He also influenced modern Quaker nonviolent action through his teaching at Pendle Hill in the 1930s.[101] Gregg captured the logic of nonviolent action by calling it "moral jiu-jitsu," an overturning of aggression that precipitates an open moment in which consciences can be reached and transformed.

Meanwhile, the marriage of the Lamb and new Jerusalem poses an integrative covenant as counter to the limited *contract* of Babylon and the Beast. Contracts between self-interested parties limit the scope and duration of obligations. By contrast, covenant is indeterminate in scope and duration, as illustrated by traditional wedding vows. Whereas contracts are defined only by the interests of the contracting parties, covenants are made in the divine presence or within a horizon of eternal values that form a coherent worldview. One is accountable to a contract, but one is faithful to a covenant, faithful in ways that inevitably transcend one's original understandings and intentions. Contracts make a party's failure liable to legal retaliation, while covenants are founded upon love, forgiveness, and new beginnings.

In sealing his covenant with his disciples, Jesus changed their status from servants to friends, a polymorphous category of relationship that adapts to all kinds of spiritual conditions and social circumstances. As his friends, the disciples' friendships are patterned by the ultimate self-giving Jesus demonstrates in laying down his life for them (John 15:1–17).

Early Friends formulated this indeterminacy of faithful relationship with the term *covenant of light*. The light as God's covenantal presence in human consciousness is indeterminate in three principle ways. First, it is *indeterminate toward God*; though Friends understood the light to be Christ, at one with the historical Jesus of Nazareth, the light's universal presence in human consciousness inevitably means that people will

82

Babylon and the Beast share the color scarlet, which matches the color of the blood of the prophets and all those who oppose them. The kings/rulers of the earth collude with this unholy union and offer their resources to the war against the Lamb. But the Lamb shall conquer (17:13–14). As noted earlier, the conspiracy of Babylon and the Beast in this age is empire's military power harnessed by the global strategic interests of capital. The conspiracy reaches acute focus in the military-industrial complex. The workings of this conspiracy are often secret, but the conspiracy itself is completely obvious—so much so that we routinely fail to notice it.

Peace/nonviolent direct action is the traditional Quaker social testimony that brings the anti-war to the military-industrial complex. Once again, our testimony is grounded in the Sermon on the Mount, where Jesus said,

> Do not resist an evildoer. But if anyone strikes you on the right cheek, turn the other also; and if anyone wants to sue you and take your coat, give your cloak as well; and if anyone forces you to go one mile, go also the second mile. (Matthew 5:39–42)

Walter Wink[99] has famously shown that these advices amount to throwing the oppressor off guard by taking his aggressive action further. These sayings of Jesus are idiomatic to his historical context but convey the logic of nonviolent practice in any age. Early Friends adopted this practice in their peaceful attack upon the unjust systems of their day. The early Quaker Lamb's War helped establish the politics of nonviolent political initiative in the early modern world.[100]

Mohandas Gandhi was influenced in part by the Sermon on the Mount when he formulated his nonviolent strategies. Richard Gregg studied in India with Gandhi and then popularized Gandhian nonviolence in America old, the helter-skelter, buccaneering economic regime bent on destruction. New Jerusalem forms as we "turn the world upside down" through denouncing the possessive individualism of consumer society and coming together to practice, model, and advocate wise stewardship on a planet that belongs to God. In all these things, we respond to the call from heaven,

> Come out of her [Babylon], my people, so that you do not take part in her sins, and so that you do not share in her plagues. (Revelation 18:4)

The market forms the middle, neutral term on this front of the anti-war. The marketplace proper should not be equated with large-scale, finance-driven capitalism. In this global, imperial phase, capitalist forces manipulate government, communications, and information toward ends often at odds with the market as such. Finance capitalism thrives as a parasitic *anti*-market, according to economic historian Giovanni Arrighi. We see this in the diverging fortunes of "Wall Street" versus "Main Street." Like civil society, the market is greatly varied, enormously creative, and morally ambiguous. Its mechanisms of supply and demand and of competitive self-interest and collaborative enterprise generate much of our culture today, for better and worse. The market can be pulled in the direction of sustainability, as seen in the current growth of organic food production. Some large corporations are ahead of governments in working to slow climate change. The economic anti-war unfolds to a great degree in the arena of the market.

The Marriage of the Lamb and the New Jerusalem: Peace

The marriage of the Lamb and the new Jerusalem envisioned by John (Revelation 21:2) is the inversion of the "deal," the conspiracy of self-interests depicted by John as Babylon riding the Beast (Revelation 17).

courage. A strong collective identity and shared commitment to simplicity can build the new Jerusalem among us.

Our movement toward simple and sustainable patterns of life is scorned by many as silly, even "bad for the economy," as if consumption were our purpose in life. But recall Nayler's comment in his 1653 *Lamentation* over England that many found early Quaker behavioral testimonies to be "small and frivolous things." He countered that

> where the conscience is kept pure it counts nothing little that Christ commands or forbids . . . and in those things you call little do we appear to be transformed into the kingdom of Christ and out of the kingdoms of the world.[97]

The testimony of simplicity grows primarily through personal and communal lifestyle choices, which then participate in larger networks of alternative economy and resource use.

These choices also inspire more politically engaged activity that challenges the laws and corporate methods that exploit poor classes and nations in order to amass greater riches for the privileged. We challenge the depletion of natural resources for profit and ever higher levels of consumption. British Friend Jonathan Dale stresses the need for local meetings and other organizations to form lifestyle sharing groups, where individuals can encourage and challenge one another to live more fully into sustainable patterns of life. But he also stresses the need for political action. For example, personal decisions about modes of transportation need to be linked with advocacy for better transportation systems.[98]

The practices of simplicity, as we observed with equality and community, are labor processes that produce coherent, sustainable *life*. They are the prefigurative politics that build the new society within the shell of the animals to labour immoderately, and with the moneys arising to him therefrom employs others in the luxuries of life, acts contrary to the gracious design of him who is the true owner of the earth; nor can any possessions, either acquired or derived from ancestors, justify such conduct.[96]

Woolman's religious socialism and environmental ethic clearly leave scope for the accumulation of wealth by those skilled in economic life. But the responsibility for wise and generous stewardship attends wealth. A tradition of socially responsible business and banking extends to this day among Friends. But in the twentieth century, corporate and financial giantism marginalized the role of small businesses and banking, leading to a migration among Friends toward the professions. Today, however, a renewal of Friends active in small businesses, organic farming, artisanship, and localist networking is reclaiming our traditional social profile with a new global awareness.

That trend brings simplicity/sustainability to the fore and may re-establish simplicity as the pre-eminent testimony of Friends, after a century of primary emphasis on the peace testimony. Simplicity is no less about peace; it is part of the larger framework of the anti-war. The exhortation from 1 Peter 2 (see the other essay of this book) takes on renewed meaning:

> *Beloved, I urge you as aliens and exiles to abstain from the desires of the flesh that wage war against the soul. Conduct yourselves honorably among the peoples, so that, though they malign you as evildoers, they may see your honorable deeds and glorify God on the day of visitation.* (vv. 11–12)

In a commodity culture that brings status to those with the latest smartphone and shame upon those who lag behind techno-fashion, the testimony of simplicity requires not only personal discernment but social our labor and experience ourselves as *God's possession.* The essay at the other end of this book explores what it means to be a *peculiar* people, God's precious possession, primarily as a collective and only secondarily as individual persons. Christians and modern Friends have tended to spiritualize that reality and sequester it from our economic life. But the more it becomes an economic and lifestyle reality, the more truly we become God's peculiar people.

Traditionally, Friends have lived into this reality through our testimony of *simplicity* or *plainness.*[95] Today, some Friends add a testimony of *sustainability* or *stewardship*, a concern for living in balance with the resources and ecosystems of the Earth, which puts a global frame on the personal and communal ethic of simplicity. Knowing ourselves as God's possession gradually shifts us from being the keepers to becoming the channels of God's material blessings. The shift from me and mine enlarges the borders of our hearts. It arouses compassion for others in their needs and the suffering of God's other creatures at human hands. John Woolman, the classic articulator of the socio-spiritual vision of traditional Friends, expresses this truth beautifully in his 1763 essay *A Plea for the Poor*:

> The Creator of the earth is the owner of it. He gave us being thereon, and our nature requires nourishment, which is the produce of it. As he is kind and merciful, we as his creatures, while we live answerable to the design of our creation, we are so far entitled to a convenient subsistence that no man may justly deprive us of it. [However, b]y the agreements and contracts of our fathers and predecessors, and by doings and proceedings of our own, some claim a much greater share of this world than others; and whilst those possessions are faithfully improved to the good of the whole, it consists with equity. But he who with a view to self-exaltation causeth some of their domestic

Recall John's comment that those who didn't bear "the mark of the Beast" were unable to buy and sell in the Roman Empire. This "mark" may have been the Emperor's and the goddess Roma's images on Roman coins. Radical Christians such as John seem to have refused to use Roman coins, as the Palestinian Zealots had and as Jesus himself may have advocated.[93] An integrated monetary system facilitated the wide range of international trade and shipping that brought commodities to Rome and other imperial cities for conspicuous consumption by the elites. (Recall the long list of commodities and precious metals John mentions in relation to Babylon's merchants and shippers.)

Here we begin to see connections with today's global capitalist regime. The international monetary exchange system is crucial to the flow of capital and commodities around the world, mostly to the advantage of the global capitalist classes—and the world's middle classes, who benefit too much to ask too many questions. Marx stressed that capitalism is first of all a form of alienated consciousness. It's not the only way human consciousness becomes spiritually and socially estranged. But in the present hypercapitalist era, it is the decisive form of alienation. The fetishization of God's creatures as *commodities*, bought and sold on the market, blocks our vision of their true "nature and virtue" (as George Fox described it in his experience of Eden[94]). We even commodify ourselves according to the value of our labor in the market. And as we increasingly define ourselves by the commodities we buy in a consumer society, we lose sight of ourselves as creatures in the sight of God. The "plastic" that allows us to buy anything anywhere begins to remold us in its own image. This alienation is the "wine of fornication" Babylon uses to besot the peoples of the earth, according to John's vision (17:2).

The *inversion* of that alienated consciousness begins as we shift our attention from the commodities *we possess* as consumers and the commodities we become through

The Anti-War

the earth. And as the inversion of Babylon, this people needs to be understood in its economic aspect in particular.

Again, the roots of this new socioeconomic reality go back to the ministry of Jesus and his Sermon on the Mount: "You are the light of the world, a city built on a hill . . . let your light shine before others, so that they may see your good works and give glory to your Father in heaven" (Matthew 5:14, 16). Jesus warned his followers that they could not serve two masters, God and wealth (6:24), that amassing material wealth would set their hearts in the wrong direction (6:19–21). He counseled them not to worry so much about material security and comforts: "Indeed your heavenly Father knows that you need all these things. But strive first for the kingdom of God and his righteousness, and all these things will be given to you as well" (6:32–33). His itinerant ministry invited an ethic of hospitality among those who received him. The story of the feeding of the five thousand implies the sharing ethic that Jesus encouraged among his followers. The kingdom appears and spreads through these social impulses, these inversions of capital accumulation.

These and other clues from his few short years of ministry indicate the kind of peasant socialism that Jesus of Nazareth initiated and encouraged. It offered a way for Palestinian society to survive the harsh taxation and repression of the Roman occupation. But his movement confronted the interests of the landowning aristocracy and the temple religion that legitimated their exploitative rule over the peasantry. The violent death that resulted from that confrontation, and the spread of the international movement that followed, easily draw our attention away from the nature and importance of the socialist movement he was initiating in Palestine during his lifetime. We don't know how it might have developed further if he had had more time.

The New Jerusalem: A Peculiar People

Just as the Beast and Babylon find their powerful synergy today in the interaction of imperial power with global capitalism, the inverse synergy unfolding in the anti-war is the interaction of the people gathered around the Lamb and their *peculiarity* as God's possession. Here we encounter Babylon's feminine counterpart, the *new Jerusalem.*

John the Palestinian Jewish Christian had seen his world pass away when the Romans destroyed Jerusalem and its temple. In Revelation, he sees a new heaven and earth appearing, with a new Jerusalem, a new holy city, adorned like a bride for her husband, the Lamb (see 21:1–22:9). He hears a voice declare that God's dwelling is now among humans; they will be his people. This "peculiar people," a people of God's own possession (as we explored in the other essay of this book), is the collective entity of the new Jerusalem. She/they are the inversion of Babylon, the overturning of her economic seduction of the peoples. Whereas Babylon was *dressed* in the precious commodities of gold, jewels, and scarlet, Jerusalem *is* precious; John describes her radiance as being like a jewel, clear as crystal. Her walls and streets are pure gold, clear as glass (clearly not the commodity). She is built upon twelve foundations, each a precious stone. She is 1,500 miles long, wide, and high. There is no temple, just the presence of God and the Lamb, who are also the only light. The river of life flows from the throne of God at the center, and the tree of life on either side of the river has leaves for the healing of the peoples of the earth, who will walk together by the light of God and the Lamb. The gates stand open, but nothing unclean can enter, simply because the city is light and the light engenders a peaceful and just society.

As the vision of a literal city in a particular place and time, these details are unrepresentable. They make sense only as the symbolic attributes of a collective people that is being gathered from among the peoples of nation. And Friends—given the polymorphous quality of relationship that our name implies—have a genius for finding allies and fellow travelers in the search for truth and the work for peace and justice. We find common cause with a wide array of religious groups, political action groups, and civil associations. Our Quaker faith and practice both influences and is influenced by these associations.

But it is important to be discerning in this regard. We can gain from light coming from new directions, but our unique Quaker ways of knowing and acting in the world must not be compromised by adopting beliefs and practices that don't really converge with ours. For example, the formation of the Movement for a New Society in the early 1970s was powerfully informed by Quaker faith and practice. Its community-based political action had a wide influence among environmental and anarchist action groups. But extraneous, popular notions of consensus eventually stifled the ability of MNS to renew its vision and action over the course of the 1980s.[91]

Civil society is a neutral realm, morally ambiguous and prone to be drawn either toward the machinations of empire (operating behind various guises) or the more organic socio-spiritual processes of the kingdom of heaven (by whatever name it is understood). But this is the ground on which our struggle plays out. It is largely pre-political and engaged with the infrastructure of empire rather than its state superstructure. Parker Palmer cogently explores this realm in two of his books, *The Company of Strangers: Christians and the Renewal of America's Public Life* and *Healing the Heart of Democracy: The Courage to Create a Politics Worthy of the Human Spirit.*[92]

John shares with the churches of Asia Minor "the tribulation and the kingdom and the patience" (1:9 KJV). These three terms describe the experience of the anti-war. First of all, the middle term, the kingdom/realm of God/heaven, is the concrete practice of the community of equals. The inversion of power and interest takes place here. Without the upside-down reality of the kingdom, our witness becomes merely oppositional, protest, anti-war. But when we *are* grounded in the kingdom, then our witness is poised between the first and third terms, tribulation and patience. Both are forms of suffering. It *may* be the outright "tribulation" of persecution, marginalization, or stigmatization by the imperial powers permeating the entire society around us. But it is *always* the "patience" of bearing with a society alienated from the healing power of God, the patience of not being understood by the dominant order, the patience that knows that "our struggle is not against enemies of blood and flesh but against the rulers, against the authorities, against the cosmic powers of this present darkness" (Ephesians 6:12).

We are called the "Religious Society of Friends." Properly used, the term "society" denotes a community of persons devoted to particular methods of knowing and to practices that express and further that knowledge. (For example, early modern scientists founded the Royal Society in England with that specific understanding of the term).[90] We should not underestimate the difference that Quaker faith and practice—rigorously enacted—makes in our outlook and our way of being within the larger society. Conversely, we should beware of a Quaker faith and practice that compromises and becomes comfortable with the dominant order (even when it appears "politically correct").

Nevertheless, we do encounter an important middle term between the Beast with its empire and the Lamb with his followers. *Civil society* is a vast and varied realm within a pluralistic and (relatively) democratic others unjustly imprisoned and brutalized by the security regime.

Lastly, the people gathered around the Lamb are the *anti-Zion*. The very nature of their shared life must oppose the militarized Zionism that unites the imperial United States with the fortress state of Israel. Again, John witnessed the self-destructive animus of Zionism two thousand years ago and envisioned the anti-Zion of the Lamb as its counter. The people that gathers around and follows the Lamb today advocates for the Palestinian people but not for the violent and corrupt organizations that claim to represent and fight for them. Likewise, the people of the Lamb collaborates with the many Israelis and American Jews whose work for peace and justice in Israel/Palestine is marginalized and discredited by empire.

All these are aspects of the anti-war, the Lamb's confrontation with the Beast, the witness of the Lamb's vanguard against the repressive power of empire. It may at times lead to outright conflict and even persecution. But even though the workings of empire grieve us, our grief becomes a surprising joy when our anti-war moves into open conflict with empire. George Fox wrote to Friends in 1663, during the worst days of their persecution,

> Sing and rejoice, ye children of the day and of the light; for the Lord is at work in this thick night of darkness that may be felt. . . . And so be of good faith and valiant for the truth: for the truth can live in jails. And fear not the loss of the fleece, for it will grow again; and follow the lamb, if it be under the beast's horns, or under the beast's heels; for the lamb shall have the victory over them all.[89]

From the Civil Rights Movement of the 1960s to environmental protest actions today, singing in jail continues to proclaim the Lamb's victory.

of power, from the pyramids of ancient Egypt and the Aztecs down to this day. Our testimony leads us to protest empire's endemic *corruption*, which inevitably attends the intersection of power and interest, inexorably producing inequality and degrading community. Our testimony is the *anti-spectacle*: there is nothing less spectacular than a Quaker meeting for worship, nothing less triumphal than a decision made in unity by the leading of the Spirit. The sensibility that develops through these practices sees through the vainglory of empire's demonstrations of national splendor and military might. The still, small voice we discern in our worship still thunders the word of the Lord as it came through the prophet Amos: "I hate, I despise your festivals, and I take no delight in your solemn assemblies . . . take away from me the noise of your songs; I will not listen to the melody of your harps. But let justice roll down like waters, and righteousness like an everflowing stream" (Amos 5:21–24).

The quiet, gentle practices of equality in community confront empire's militarization of domestic police and the global "police" role of its military. In contrast to violently defended interests, equality in community creates mutual *sanctuary* among its participants, an *anti-prison* that exposes the brutalization and mass incarceration that sustain empire. Quaker prison ministries and work for prison reform arise from the sanctuary we experience together and extend toward offenders and victims alike.

The wisdom of God revealed through our silent waiting together is the *anti-intelligence*. It sees what surveillance cannot detect, what torture cannot extract, what "big data" can never amass. It "discerns the thoughts and intentions of the heart. And before him no creature is hidden, but all are naked and laid bare" (Hebrews 4:12–13). Consequently, it draws Friends in the United States out of their largely white, middle-class social ghettos to align with African Americans and

They are *gathered* by his light in their consciences and they *follow* him by the leadings of the same light. In his early ministry in Galilee, Jesus taught his followers, "You are the light of the world, a city built on a hill. . . . Let your light shine before others, so that they may see your good works and give glory to your Father in heaven" (Matthew 5:14, 16). In Quaker practice, this gathering and following develop through regular personal practices of spiritual devotion and the rhythm of Quaker meetings. The "gathered" meeting for worship is a felt reality as Christ moves freely among surrendered souls, speaks through human instruments, and knits the body of Friends together into a covenantal community of equals. It is further developed through worshipful meetings for business, where individuals submit personal interest and power to the wisdom of the group as a whole, as it is forged into unity by the Spirit. Over years of seeking and doing truth together, the community of Friends subverts the reflexes that routinely create division, inequality, and injustice in the wider society. To be sure, the covenant community is constantly challenged to live further into its calling to be inclusive and egalitarian. This people is always flawed, imperfectly embodying its calling. But plain speaking, forgiveness, reconciliation, and new beginnings are at the heart of covenant life.

The traditional Quaker "testimonies" of *equality* and *community* offer lived expression to these covenantal qualities.[88] Sustained movement toward greater equality, which becomes personally meaningful in community, constitutes our gathering around the Lamb and manifests Mount Zion in time and space. Testimonies *testify* to the truth as we know it in Christ, the light. The testimonies are productive labor, whether economic or not. They produce healthy, intimate *life* in the midst of the alienated and unequal social norms of the Dragon's thrall.

But our testimony inevitably places us in conflict with the machinery of empire, which has glorified hierarchies patterns among us. Here we revisit the title and structure of this book's inverse essay, "Peace Finds the Purpose of a Peculiar People." But coming to these terms from the opposite direction, we will learn new things from them. We will explore this inverted socio-spiritual experience in terms of Jesus' teaching to his nascent community in the Sermon on the Mount (Matthew 5–7) and the Quaker social testimonies. Let us begin in the upper-left corner.

The Lamb and the Gathered People

Recall that immediately after the visions of the Beast and the False Prophet, John sees the Lamb standing on Mount Zion with a vanguard of 144,000 gathered around him (Revelation 14:1). As a Jewish refugee from Palestine, John had seen the earthly Zion of Jerusalem and its temple razed by the Romans in response to a Jewish revolt. He had seen its people slaughtered or else carried off into slavery by the tens of thousands. By contrast, the Zion of this vision is a social space not defined by geography, not contested by political power or defended by violent force. It is a people not defined by ethnic identity or delimited by ceremonial rites. The Lamb, "slaughtered from the foundation of the world" (Revelation 13:8), is both Jesus of Nazareth, crucified by the Empire, and the inward Christ, repressed and crucified wherever humans choose power and personal interest over the gentle promptings of love and reconciliation. "The world" is indeed "founded" upon mechanisms of competition and conflict between vying interests and powers. Empire is an acute form of these mechanisms, raised to geopolitical dimensions. The Beast/Empire exerts power over all the peoples (13:7). To the extent that they think and operate by the Empire's principles of power and interest, the Beast controls them.

But the *people* gathered by the Lamb on heavenly Mount Zion "follow the Lamb wherever he goes" (14:5).

The format of this book manifests physically the ironic relationship between the Lamb and the Dragon and between their socio-spiritual dynamics. The book has to be inverted and turned around in order to move from one reality to the other. The book's structure and concept are intended to function like a good joke, where the punchline comes from an unexpected but revealing angle. Our orientation determines what we see. Our challenge is to maintain a double perspective even if we cannot see "both sides of the coin" at the same time.

Before we move on, another feature of Figure 2 needs to be noted. The perennial danger of apocalyptic thought is that its strong dichotomies can degenerate into sheer *dualism*, as if Christ and the Beast were equal forces of the same nature. The millenarian, speculative caricature of apocalyptic thought that dominates much Christian use of Revelation falls into that trap. But not only are these inverse forms of power; our experience, particularly in a pluralistic society, tells us that their relationship is not dualistic, an absolute ethical binary.

Modern, secular society is highly complex and morally ambiguous. Accordingly, the treatment here poses an *intermediate* square between the dichotomous squares of Dragon vs. Lamb, suggesting a neutral, morally ambiguous realm at each corner. Thus, whereas the outer square of the Dragon and its forces is defined by power and interest as they are typically brokered by contracts of limited scope, interest, and duration, the inner square of the Lamb and his community is defined by truth and love bound together in covenantal faithfulness. But *between* these oppositional realities, much of our social experience is more neutral. It can be pulled in either direction, toward integrative wholeness or entropic destruction.

Finally, the inverted reality of the Lamb and his followers is not to be simply asserted in dogmatic terms. It starts with the nature of our *experience* in the light of Christ and the personal and social *practices* that it

Part 4

The Anti-War

We now move into the realm that the essay at the other end of this book explores according to the internal logic of the community of faith. However, coming to it from this angle, from our exploration of the Dragon's powers of entropy and destruction, the Lamb and his community constitute a striking *inversion*. In the first century, those who lived according to the Roman Empire's reality complained that Christians were "turning the world upside down" (Acts 17:6). In the English Commonwealth of the seventeenth century, ruling class interests made the same complaint against Quakers and other radicals.[86]

Indeed, from *within* that inverted reality, George Fox wrote to Friends in 1653 that the cross of Christ (the light's revelation) "overturns the world in the heart . . . [and] where the world is standing, the cross is not lived in. But dwelling in the cross to the world, here the love of God is shed abroad in the heart, and the way is opened."[87]

This is crucial for Christians, Friends, and others converging in the present struggle. If we mirror the logic and match the tactics of the present system, we are defeated from the start. The *anti-war* of the Lamb and his community is an inversion of the violent social order and actions of the Dragon and his forces. At the same time, if we stay within the comforting dynamics of the community of faith, that sanctuary becomes a self-referential prison. Our social concerns remain a parlor conversation that never really grapples with the system everywhere around it.

Capitalism, Empire, and the Military-Industrial Complex

That strange text is the map that helps us find our ground and hold it against the monstrous forces of this present age.

wielding economic power. The all-pervading security imperative of today's capitalist empire inspires threat-management strategies that build racist assumptions into law enforcement and skews the judicial system against minorities, whose otherness threatens European American normative status.[85] These processes—especially when unconscious or unacknowledged—do undermine democratic processes and reverse political reforms. The hyper-monetarization of electoral politics and lobbying in recent decades only exacerbates these tendencies.

Some analysts reason that the American case cannot be called fascist because it hasn't made use of thugs intimidating dissenters in the streets, as occurred in Nazi Germany and Fascist Italy in the 1930s. But the corporate-controlled media manufacture acquiescence pervasively and subliminally through the constant framing and filtering of news and cultural conversation. And of course, the older fascist tradition does continue in the violently repressive tactics of some police against African and Latino American communities.

As Benito Mussolini himself remarked in *The Political and Social Doctrine of Fascism*, 1932, "Whoever has seen in the religious politics of the Fascist regime nothing but mere opportunism has not understood that Fascism besides being a system of government is also, and above all, a system of thought." The fascist religion of the False Prophet's blasphemy is not a mere ploy but is essential to the maintenance of imperial order.

Again, the most potent ideology is one that doesn't seem ideological at all, just commonsensical. The fascist religion of empire today must be confronted and countered with a religious language that offers a radically different understanding of *the same religious traditions and texts utilized by fascist ideologues today*. "Alternative" religions and spiritualities generally offer only personal solace and social escape. The Book of Revelation is a prime text of American fascist religion.

In the United States today, the fascist formula has been revised but remains essentially the same. Given today's highly technologized warfare, surveillance, and intelligence, "military citizenship" is imposed more efficiently on all by federal income taxes collected for "national defense" (currently 60 percent of federal discretionary spending) than by military conscription. The "permanent war economy," entrenched in the United States since the Korean War years, has accomplished the fascist agenda more pervasively than the Nazis ever managed. And though overt racism has been largely repressed since the civil rights era, the systemic racism of America's criminal justice and penal systems has created a "growing and permanent under-caste" of African Americans through the mass incarceration of black men. As Michelle Alexander makes clear in *The New Jim Crow*,[83] African Americans are marginalized from the economic and political mainstream as effectively today as they were in the South's old "Jim Crow" regime.

Manning Marable's *How Capitalism Underdeveloped Black America* quotes from Walter Rodney's *How Europe Underdeveloped Africa*:

> Fascism is a deformity of capitalism. It heightens the imperialist tendency towards domination which is inherent in capitalism, and it safeguards the principle of private property. At the same time, fascism immeasurably strengthens the institutional racism already bred by capitalism. . . . Fascism reverses the political gains of the bourgeois democratic system, such as free elections, equality before the law, parliaments, etc.[84]

Perhaps capitalism simply indulges racism rather than actively breeding it, as Rodney charges. Capitalism's one value is the dissolving power of money. But that apparent value neutrality nevertheless empowers the racist, sexist, and other motives harbored by those

World War II, I have long considered the term "fascist" to be a "meaningless epithet" slung indiscriminately against one's political opponents. The term evokes images of jack-booted Nazi soldiers goose-stepping through the streets of Berlin. But as early as 1980, Bertram Gross coined the term "friendly fascism"[81] to describe America's version of the blasphemy that overcame Germany and Italy in the 1930s. Gross's book came out as Ronald Reagan rose to the American presidency, riding a wave of neoconservative backlash against the progressive politics of the 1960s and '70s. Gross recognized that an economic, political, and military superstructure was taking decisive control of the nation. Reagan's soft-spoken, soothing manner was nothing like the strident affect of Hitler or Mussolini. But the senescent film actor proved an effective talking statue for the sophisticated neoconservative strategists huddled behind him.

Meanwhile, the continuing stream of World War II films has kept the category "fascist" and the image of palpable evil at a safe distance in time and space from American self-awareness. American geniality and sentimentality seem the very opposite of fascism. Yet, as Henri Nouwen notes, sentimentality and violence are two sides of the same currency of illusion.[82] Hitler could be moved to tears by a small child, and he dearly loved his pets. Americans today are deeply immersed in a society of spectacle, awash in images and illusions, massaged by the bathos and pathos of non-stop entertainment and diversion.

The fascist movement began during World War I, when total war had erased the difference between citizen and combatant. Fascists concluded that industrialized warfare had rendered liberal democracy obsolete and imposed "military citizenship" as everyone's role in one form or another. Aggressive imperialism was the only route to national renewal. The fascists borrowed some ideas from the socialists but replaced class struggle with international conflict and racial scapegoating tactics.

Fascism

The False Prophet personifies John's insight into the cult of Caesar-worship in ancient Rome. The False Prophet encouraged the popular view of the Empire as an invincible power and of the emperor as "savior," "lord," and guarantor of world peace and prosperity. Monumental architecture celebrating military might magnified imperial grandeur. "Talking" statues of Caesar dazzled the gullible.

This relates to the way early Friends viewed the enfranchised clergy of the state-sponsored church in seventeenth-century England. The clergy spread a veil of religious mystification and ideological justification over coercive religion and state power. In turn, the state enforced the collection of tithes and other forms of financial support for its established church and clerical class. Early Friends charged that coerced faith alienates the human conscience from the presence and teaching of Christ, the light within, and thereby engenders other forms of social alienation, inequality, and violence.

The False Prophet today takes many forms, many of them secular, right-wing political groups with powerful lobbying organizations and political action committees. But John's vision of the False Prophet's blasphemy finds its most acute expression today in the overtly *religious* justifications of the Christian Right in America. Conservative churches routinely bless both capitalism and militarism. Right-wing evangelists such as John Hagee endorse American military support for the state of Israel as the fulfillment of their violent, millenarian interpretations of the Book of Revelation. It is important to remember that these churches in America are highlighted in the media. Major sectors of American churches do not endorse these politics, but somehow these are not deemed "newsworthy."

The Religious Right is indeed large, powerful, and well organized. Like George Orwell, writing shortly after expands beyond military, terrorist, and cyber threats to include oil production and other resource issues.

Given its massive investment in military preparedness, the nation's overwhelming military capability sometimes makes violence America's first resort, despite the continuing "just war" rhetoric that it is the last resort. "Humanitarian intervention" in violent situations around the globe enlists moral support for "police" action by the United States and its allies. Nongovernmental organizations and even the World Council of Churches have felt compelled to collaborate with or to endorse military solutions to human rights crises.[80]

Since the end of military conscription in 1972, the voluntary basis of military service has made the human costs of war less disturbing to most Americans. And the careful vetting and "embedding" of journalists with military units in combat zones keeps the most appalling realities of war from the public eye. Nevertheless, Eisenhower's experienced observation remains true: "War is costly, brutal and stupid." That is not apparent to young recruits who join for truly virtuous and honorable purposes, risking life, limb, and mental health for their country. But, at the time of this writing, the suicide rate among American veterans of the Afghan and Iraq wars is at twenty-two per week. The horrors American soldiers have witnessed, suffered, or committed remain largely hidden or abstract to the vast majority of us. Even for some in the military, war's horrors remain remote. The guidance of smart bombs and attack drones around the world from comfortable control centers in the United States merges with the militaristic violence of computer games played on comfortable sofas at home.

But even with all these synergistic forces and trends already undergirding the military-industrial complex, the Dragon's thrall also generates the more overt ideological dimension of empire that John envisioned.

underserved sectors of American society. In part, this "freedom" expresses the pure liquidity of money that operates as an implicit ideology in postmodernity, as noted earlier. Money buys the freedom to follow whatever desire and buy protection against whatever perceived threat. It is highly synergistic with the cyber-technology that allows one to explore and purchase anything in any direction, thanks to the World Wide Web—an invention of the American military. The limitless possibilities of technology only intensify the consumer's sense of need. When Apple's iPad went on the market, a man in a long line was asked by an interviewer why he wanted to buy one. He replied, "I don't know yet, but I'll find out when I get it." The Web and the Internet create the instantaneous Now that captures the entire globe in an omnipresent Here. This is another aspect of the merging of inside and outside in today's global empire. The effect can be a euphoric sense of wide-open possibility one moment and a claustrophobic sense of captivity the next.

Meanwhile, population pressures, resource depletion, and the dependence of so much of today's life upon the electrical grid induces a pervasive anxiety for *security*. Nietzsche identified this tendency in European modernity even in the late nineteenth century. This anxiety pervades society today more than ever[78] and plays into the purposes of militarism, generating broad, unquestioning political support among a fearful populace. Consequently, most Americans have been willing to turn their heads and ignore the U.S. use of torture in the name of national security. Cultural theorist Brian Massumi[79] argues that "threat" in contemporary society becomes an ambient affect, an operative logic that creates its own reality. The U.S. "war on terror" was first declared by Richard Nixon in the early 1970s. It has reshaped American consciousness to its purposes ever since. In American political discourse, the motif of national security confronted within each of us as much as in the power structures that reach so far above our heads.

The old cannons, tanks, and other military hardware that decorate the grounds of countless county courthouses, city parks, and other public areas across the United States bespeak the unquestioned militarism of the American ethos. Wouldn't old tractors and harvesting machines around an Indiana courthouse better celebrate the true strength of that county?

The gun fetishism of the National Rifle Association's membership further manifests the spiritual miasma of the military-industrial complex. It's a psychological complex as much as a political and economic one. For example, the background story of Adam Lanza of the Sandy Hook school massacre reveals an obsession with guns, abetted by his mother's racist fears of uprisings spilling out from American cities.[77] The successful NRA campaign to fend off even minimal gun control legislation after Sandy Hook reveals how fully it controls the U.S. Congress. The NRA's rhetoric of defending American freedom obliquely expresses its deeper motivations and financial backing: right-wing, anti-government, quasi-militia groups arming against the federal government and racial minorities. Ammunition sales soared after the election of Barack Obama in 2008.

The militia mentality goes all the way back to the violent hijacking of America's colonial nonviolent resistance against imperial Britain in 1775, noted earlier. It is also tinged with the abiding anti-federal sentiments of the Civil War's southern Confederacy. Thus, the spirituality of the military-industrial complex even produces some effects that are counter to empire itself—but tinged with white supremacist, patriarchal, and other regressive ideological orientations.

Thus, the undefined "freedom" the NRA and other violent groups claim to "defend" is clearly not a socially progressive agenda to liberate oppressed and

That drunkenness among Wall Street's self-proclaimed "masters of the universe" led up to the economic collapse of 2008. That power is both economically and politically coercive. It is both Babylon and the Beast. Since 2008, the distance between Wall Street and Main Street, between the finance-driven economy and the rest of the market, has continued to grow. While the rest of the economy has struggled to recover, the stock market and derivatives have soared to new heights, notwithstanding the warnings from leading economists that we are building toward another meltdown. President Obama's appointment of the same economists who earlier led the nation and the world into the recession only confirms the powerful synergy between empire and capital.

Military-Industrial Complex

This is a complex term that is more than the sum of these two elements as I have portrayed them thus far. It takes on a life of its own in the military-industrial complex, whose influence is far-reaching and subtle. Fourteen years into the war in Afghanistan, the leading grower of the opium poppy, the price of heroin on U.S. streets has fallen to record lows in constant dollars. What's the connection? Perhaps it is similar to the connection between the invasion of Iraq in 2003 and Vice President Dick Cheney's connections with Halliburton, a leading American contractor in Iraq during and after the war. The military-industrial complex supplies the aphrodisiac that continues to arouse the economy and inspire an adventurous foreign policy.

No doubt, some conspiracies really do exist. But the logic of empire creates synergies that have a life of their own, without the necessity of secret cabals in every case. Hence, Eisenhower's point that the military-industrial complex is a spiritual as well as political and economic problem is well made. The power of Babylon riding the Beast pervades everything and everyone. It must be

Money has long been recognized as corrosive to all other values. For example, Jesus posed the choice between serving God or Mammon. But world monetarism has taken this ancient dilemma to significantly new dimensions. The nonstop spectacle projected by the media plays constantly on fear and desire through daily doses of sensational news punctuated by relentless advertising. The corporations that control the media filter and frame what we see and hear according to their own large-scale economic interests and political preferences. As Debord emphasized long ago, in the spectacular society, only what appears exists. An element of glamor attends the media-projected image. It draws us toward personalities, consumer products, and environments. "Glamor" traditionally connoted a bewitching beauty or charm. In today's mediated society, it is less a matter of the uncanny than the canny strategies of advertising and the canny strategies consumers devise to acquire the glamorous, to become glamorous.[76] Glamor, enchanting all sectors of society through the penetrating liquidity of money, becomes a powerful force of corruption.

Anyone who follows these trends with critical concern can add more detail to the few broad strokes of this portrait. But the point in this essay is to move beyond symptoms to the systemic, beyond blaming neoconservatives, the 1 percent super-rich, or climate-change deniers, in order to confront the apocalyptic dimension of these phenomena. The point is to move beyond liberal laments to a stark, world-ending revelation and stance of resistance—the anti-war.

We behold here Babylon's arrogant glory. Babylon degrades the covenant that binds us in faithful relationship with God, with one another, and with the creation. Babylon beckons us to settle for an adulterous quid pro quo deal with the narrowed scope and limited liability of a contract. Money is the wine with which Babylon makes the nations drunk, but what makes Babylon drunk is the power to roll over all opposition.

mass society in his 1967 classic, *Society of the Spectacle*.[75]

Capitalism

The reader may have already noted that the phenomena we have just described are as much economic as political. We now move diagonally to the lower right corner of the square and examine more closely the synergy between empire and the global capitalist enterprise, a dynamic in the thrall of the Beast and Babylon. As noted earlier, with the floating currency exchange system that began in 1973, the financial sector—stocks, futures, derivatives, etc.—dominates the system. Even corporations that produce and trade in actual commodities become preoccupied with mergers and takeovers rather than production. Banking and finance become an anti-market, feeding parasitically upon the real market of commodities and labor.

With monetarism dominating the system, money itself—pure liquidity and the limitless options it provides—becomes the unacknowledged ideology of capitalism. Anecdotal confirmation was revealed in the Enron scandal in 2001. The accounting masterminds who were finding ever more clever ways to hide corporate debt on weekdays flew to Las Vegas on the weekends to gamble. The most effective ideology is one that doesn't seem ideological at all but simply the way things are.

And so the actions of the Federal Reserve and other central banks around the world take center stage. A nuanced remark from one of them sends stock markets up or down, with ripple effects throughout the economy and the market-driven culture. Society wavers in the balance of desire and fear: that is, the desire for more commodities and the fear of any economic, political, or environmental setback that might lead to outcomes ranging from a minor recession to a breakdown of the increasingly tenuous, over-leveraged system.

jailed or imprisoned in the United States. Although the state endorses no racist ideology, persisting racist attitudes are readily folded into its powers of law enforcement and its penal codes.

Corruption—moral, judicial, and political—is also systemic in empire.[73] Polybius noted it in ancient Rome. Domination by weaponized power leads the peoples of the earth to conclude, as John quotes in Revelation 13:4, "Who is like the Beast and who can fight against it?" Hardened cynicism ensues. Those who can gain some form of leverage within the empire will use it for personal advantage and gain, as seen in countless examples at every level of U.S. government and in the nations of the world. Corruption, in every sense, is the chief complaint of Islamists against the West and serves as a primary motivation of those joining terrorist organizations, as recently shown by Sarah Chayes in *Thieves of State: Why Corruption Threatens Global Security*.[74]

Spectacle magnifies the power of empire and enthralls its peoples. We noted earlier the Roman penchant for monumental architecture celebrating imperial victories and symbolizing imperial splendor. These were augmented by spectacles of combat and death in the arenas. Today's empire utilizes modern media to project spectacle in many forms, such as sporting events, television programs, and movies. Hollywood churns out blockbuster action films, replete with computerized special effects and spectral violence, for an audience that is often larger outside the United States than within. You don't have to understand English in order to be wowed by large explosions. All this numbs people to the violence of the system, rendering them passive, pliant factotums to the bidding of empire. Mass culture erodes the power of communities to nurture character and moral commitment. Howard Brinton raised some of these concerns as early as 1948. The French Situationist Guy Debord identified spectacle as a key dynamic of territorial incursions from without, is a power easily harnessed by special interests for unjust purposes: economic advantage, racist or sexist biases, etc. Such purposes are *not* divinely ordained, though the state may allege that they are. Moreover, when a state becomes powerful enough economically and militarily to conquer or otherwise dominate other states, it becomes an empire.

As suggested in the preceding section, we have moved into a form of empire in the past half-century that is premised upon dominant American military and economic power but operates by a consensus of states and by economic interests with multiple centers around the globe. It includes capitalist elites even in poor countries. Here we can speak of empire as manifesting the qualities John identified with the Beast in Revelation 13. John describes the Beast as having authority over all peoples, nations, and languages. Certainly, today's empire has a reach far greater than that of the Roman Empire of John's day.

Military campaigns and police actions begin to merge because the difference between inside and outside blurs, given empire's global reach.[72] The United States becomes "policeman of the world," while municipal police departments within the United States are increasingly militarized. Their purchase of military hardware from the U.S. Department of Defense enables police to dominate the streets with escalating levels of violent force. That force is deemed necessary owing to the unregulated gun trade within the United States (the less recognized endemic dimension of the military-industrial complex). Meanwhile, the FBI operates outside the United States in the war on terror, while the CIA and NSA penetrate increasingly within. Thus, war/police action becomes systemic—not the exception but permanent and pervasive. War becomes a guiding metaphor in various realms: sports, poverty, drugs, terror, etc. Under these conditions, civil liberties erode and rates of incarceration rise, with 2.2 million now violence, like that of a bomb. We could also call it a centrifugal force. The forces of the Dragon are destructive, death-dealing; they pull life apart and draw us into various forms of alienation from God, from ourselves, from each other, from the creation. When George Fox deals with the question of evil,[71] he characterizes it as "deceit," delusion, and "out of the truth." In a sense, then, evil doesn't really exist. But through delusion, desire, envy, and competition something teases our hearts and minds out from truth, away from our communion with God and our wiser ways. As we give evil our energy and attention, evil becomes a real and powerful force.

Fox uses biblical terms such as Satan, devil, or serpent when writing about evil in personal experience. He reserves the term Dragon for social, structural forms of evil. This essay is premised on the idea that there is a recurring structure, a gestalt of social evil that John described in ancient, mythic terms in the first century, which early Friends adapted to their seventeenth-century circumstances and which may give us insight into our predicament today. From an apocalyptic perspective, then, we can see that this destructive, entropic force is pulling society apart today. It is the final horizon for understanding the military-industrial complex in its overall formation and the challenge it poses for integrative peacemaking today.

The Second Outermost Square

This square includes elements introduced in the preceding historical background section. We begin in the upper left corner with *state/empire*. The territorial state, addressed in the other essay of this book as "civil authority," is "ordained by God" in its vocation to restrain evil, to provide sufficient social order that people are not preyed upon and their good intentions may succeed. But the power of "the sword," both to punish wrongdoing within its borders and to fend off

Capitalism, Empire, and the Military-Industrial Complex

that John was not "predicting" the conflict of our age twenty centuries after he lived. Rather, the structure of John's insight into his own times helps *reveal* the conflict of our age, just as it helped early Friends clarify the nature of their historic conflict.

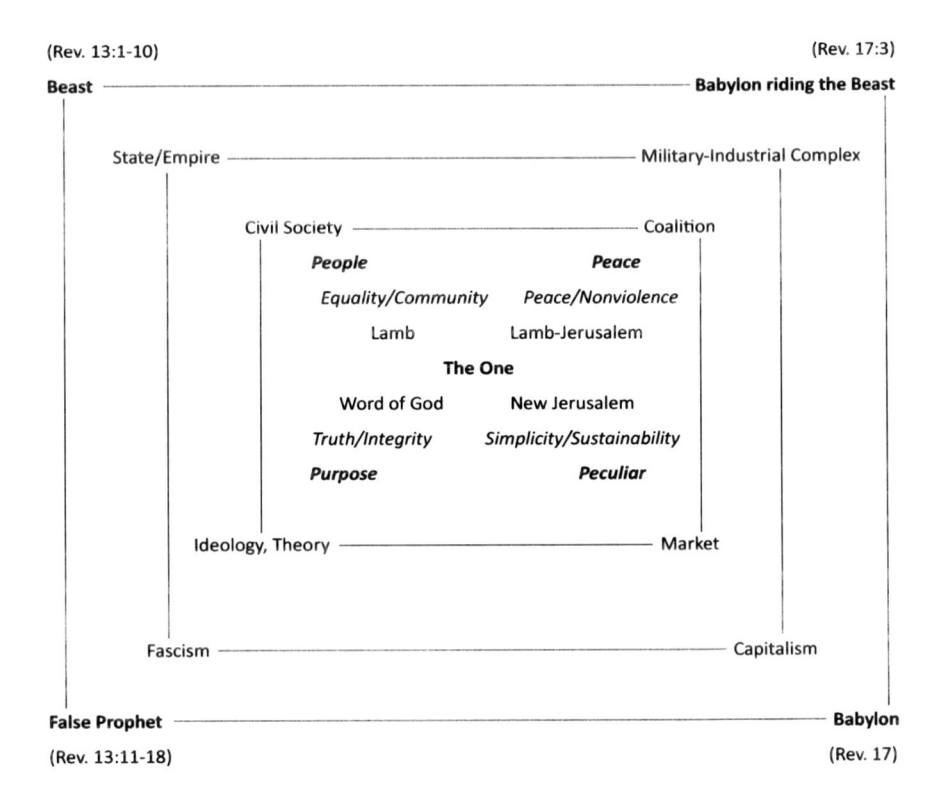

Figure 2: Engaging the Dragon in Anti-War

The Outermost Square

This outer square is the one discussed in the earlier section on Revelation. The four forces of the Dragon are forces of evil, which we might alternately describe as spiritual forces of entropy: chaos, life-annihilating

51

postmodernity, the spatial grid of multiple identities and affinities has eclipsed the temporal sense of linear direction. The Internet has become postmodernity's mode and metaphor.

We find ourselves in a framework akin to the Book of Revelation, which is less a prediction of linear history than a kaleidoscope of visions evoking the deep structures of contradiction between the Roman Empire and the early Christian movement. We have explored Revelation as a *post-ancient* text; that is, it lays out the fatal contradictions of the ancient, pagan world in the advent of the Christian movement. We then examined the early Quaker use of Revelation in framing their Lamb's War conflict with established, coercive religion. That movement, arising at an early phase of modernity, contributed to the final deconstruction of the feudal social order. Now, in our postmodern context, Revelation may again help structure the terms of a more prophetic Quaker peace testimony, raising our episodic and reactive anti-war spasms to the level of a programmatic *anti-war*. Certainly, Friends are already engaged piecemeal in parts of this anti-war. But our engagement with Revelation here aims to bring these scattered efforts to a more integrative self-awareness, intention, and action.

Empire Today

The military-industrial complex may be charted in its overall configuration within a global economy in terms of the square established in the preceding study of Revelation (see Figure 1). Figure 2 (below) adds the ways in which those gathered around the Lamb engage the forces of the Dragon in anti-war. In addition, the four key elements of the other essay of this book, "Peace Finds the Purpose of a Peculiar People," are configured with the Lamb. Finally, the traditional Quaker testimonies are aligned as our practices in this nonviolent struggle. Again, it is important to emphasize attacks upon the World Trade Center and the Pentagon in 2001. Islamic revolution has henceforth helped sustain the basis for military Keynesianism through the wars in Afghanistan and Iraq and the war on terror in general.

Michael Hardt and Antonio Negri[69] argue that although today's empire has developed through American initiatives, it is not an American empire as such. Certainly, the United States enjoys a privileged position as the largest economy and the lone military superpower. But given the array of powerful capitalist centers around the world, today's empire doesn't coincide definitively with the United States. The United States is rather the strongest partner in a variety of economic alliances such as the G20 and military alliances such as NATO. The presidency of George W. Bush veered toward a more unilateral American leadership, but the Obama presidency has re-established the more multilateral approach that Bill Clinton had advanced.

Today's postcolonial, global economy draws human resources worldwide into a consolidating market system. This system generates a cultural logic no longer based upon Eurocentric, androcentric, or Christian assumptions. The resulting multicultural, feminist, and secular/interfaith ethos is sometimes labeled postmodern. Modernity, a European political, economic, and cultural project, was quite successful in conquering and colonizing much of the world. But it also generated two world wars of such devastation that the American regime emerged in its place. As Fredric Jameson[70] suggests, the postmodern world is certainly still "modern." But the world system now juggles multiple modernities that are inflected with different cultural traditions, political programs, and economic networks. The confident modernist trajectory of historical "progress" is now eclipsed by a technocratic concern for appropriate "processes," the optimal interaction and management of differences. In the dollar. In 1973, the United States abandoned the gold standard and initiated a system of flexible, floating exchange rates between all currencies, immediately creating enormous global liquidity. Currency trading quickly surpassed commodity production and trade as the determining economic sector. A new global capitalist revolution was underway, one in which corporate finance and banking became the driving force.

Meanwhile, Nixon's devaluation of the dollar (the currency normally used by all nations to pay for oil) had alienated Arab leaders from the United States. They were further antagonized by American policy in the Middle East after the Yom Kippur War of October 1973. The following December, the Organization of Petroleum Exporting Countries (OPEC) quadrupled the price of oil to $11.65 per barrel, accelerating inflationary pressures around the world and sending non-oil-producing poor nations into crisis.

Thus, by 1974 a new phase in the relation between capitalist interests and territorial states with military power was emerging. Ronald Reagan's ascent to the American presidency in 1980 brought a neoconservative economic agenda that aligned itself with the new corporate and finance-driven regime. Moreover, Reagan's anti-communist ideology renewed the arms race and the economic strategy of military Keynsianism, initiating a second cold war. The Federal Reserve raised interest rates, which drew investment capital from around the world to the United States but further impoverished third-world nations. The collapse of the Soviet empire a decade later left the United States as the sole superpower and allowed the integration of the former Soviet states into the global capitalist regime.

Meanwhile, American policy in the Middle East helped spark militant Islamist ideologies, beginning with the Iranian revolution in 1979 and spawning ever more violent and terrorist mutations in succeeding years. The phenomenon reached full symbolic impact with the

States would also find itself exerting its military strength to serve the neocolonial purposes of overseas investment around the world.

King's integrative vision is striking. Again, the interaction of economic and military interests is especially important to note. Western capitalism has thrived through the interaction of capitalist interests and territorial states with strong militaries, in shifting reconfigurations since the Italian Renaissance.[68] Conquest and colonization built the wealth of imperialist Europe over several centuries, as it had the Roman Empire. But in the postwar era, European nations shrugged off their colonies as a net loss. American world leadership asserted itself through economic clout and military dominance without needing to conquer and colonize outright.

A new kind of empire was in the making. The period 1968–74 marks the crucial transition to this new regime. The Tet Offensive at the start of 1968 began to reveal the nature and costs of a war the United States would not win. Years later, Secretary of War Robert McNamara reflected that he and other U.S. leaders kept imposing a Cold War template upon a conflict the North Vietnamese insisted was a war of independence. Thus, Vietnamese aspirations slowly forced a third-world perspective upon the two-world consciousness of both American and Soviet imperialism.

Meanwhile, corporations viewed the Third World with a different set of aspirations. Decolonialization in the 1950s and 1960s had opened developing countries to more free-flowing commercial investment. Massive corporate profits began to accumulate in accounts outside the United States. The Bretton Woods monetary system, which had established the U.S. dollar as the reserve currency for international trade based on fixed rates of exchange, broke down. The run on the dollar spiraled until Johnson's successor, Richard Nixon, halted the conversion of dollars into gold and devalued magazine pondered, "Is the military about to take over U. S. science lock, stock, and barrel, calling the tune for U. S. universities and signing up the best scientists for work fundamentally aimed at military results?"[65] Meanwhile, companies with defense contracts spread so broadly around the nation that military-industrial interests infiltrated an overwhelming majority of Congressional districts, ensuring high levels of military spending and aid down to this day. Given these interactions, one might more accurately describe this phenomenon as a military-industrial-technological-academic-congressional complex. Each of the hyphenated terms strengthens the others.

In January 1961, on his way out of the White House, the five-star general and commander-in-chief of U.S. armed forces Dwight Eisenhower warned the American public of the dangers of the military-industrial complex. He portrayed it as "a permanent armaments industry of vast proportions," a "defense establishment" pervading "the very structure of our society" with an influence that is "economic, political, even spiritual," with "grave implications" that could "endanger our liberties or democratic processes."[66] The purpose of this essay is now to explore that structure in each of those aspects.

Eisenhower's successor, John F. Kennedy, flanked by stalwart cold warriors as advisors, further abetted the military-industrial complex as he accelerated the arms race and ventured America's first steps into Vietnam. Kennedy's successor, Lyndon Johnson, blundered deeper into Vietnam, causing military spending to soar still further. Civil Rights Movement leader Martin Luther King Jr., in his "Beyond Vietnam" speech of April 1967, set out a detailed critique of the war and issued a prophetic warning regarding the future outworkings of the nation's present course.[67] He noted that, by inheriting from France a European imperialist war, the United States had compromised its standing as a beacon of freedom and human progress among the nations. If these trends were not reversed, the United

inevitably spreads to other areas, will quickly
put an end to our kind of democracy.[62]

With prescient clarity, Brinton saw the pathological
interaction of the systemic and the personal in the
postwar regime, whereas most Americans simply
exulted in renewed peace and prosperity.

Roosevelt had envisioned the emergence of a one-world
system after the war. But Soviet expansionism and the
Chinese Communist Revolution of 1949 led Britain's
Winston Churchill and America's Harry Truman to
frame a two-world scenario in which renewed military
might would be essential to counter the threat of world
Communism. Sustained high levels of defense spending
would also meet economists' concerns to maintain
capital flows and avert economic stagnation. The
postwar U.S. Congress had initially aimed to wind down
military appropriations, but the Korean conflict
stampeded them into massive military spending and
aid, a trend that continued through the 1950s and 60s.

The interaction of economic stimulus and militarism
fueled the highest rate of economic growth in world
history. But it also initiated the phenomenon that
economist Seymour Melman named in 1976 "the
permanent war economy."[63] A "military Keynesianism"
sought to stimulate global economic growth through
military spending.[64] Given the spectacular economic
growth of the Cold War era, few Americans were
sufficiently discerning, unself-interested, or courageous
to question the morality of an economy on steroids.
(The American Friends Service Committee's 1955
booklet *Speak Truth to Power* offered an early,
integrative critique.) Moreover, the consumer behemoth
known as the baby boom generation both fed and fed off
of these trends.

The military-capitalist equation exerted its logic in all
directions. Military funding was already driving
university research to such an extent in 1946 that *Time*

decisive in the war, would act as leader of this economic order. In the Marshall Plan, designed to rebuild the nations that had been devastated by the war, Franklin Roosevelt envisioned a global extension of his New Deal economics.

Meanwhile, military conscription was extended beyond the end of the war. Howard Brinton, Dean of Studies at Pendle Hill, the Quaker study center outside Philadelphia, recognized the long-term militarist trend even before the end of the war. He observed that fear was a basic motive for a peacetime military policy. Americans readily admitted to that. However, the other motive, imperialistic expansion, was not even discussed. By contrast, nonviolent love of enemies is an ethic grounded in courage, not fear. "Our nation must soon arrive at its decision. Shall we go to the drill-master to find the way to peace or to Him who said, 'My peace I give unto you, not as the world giveth?'"[60] In 1948, Brinton asked larger social questions for the postwar era, such as, "How can intellectual and moral judgment be developed in the face of mass pressure?" He saw an old problem becoming more acute: mass communications and modern methods of manipulating public opinion and desires through psychological techniques would weaken the inner life. He noted that "increased knowledge of human psychology has placed in the hands of a few a method and means of subjugating men more potent than guns or prison walls."[61] Urbanization, militarism, corporate giantism, endless gadgetry, and other developments

> tend to produce a mass-minded type of individual wide open to suggestions of all sorts, an easy victim of advertising and other forms of mass-pressure. As inner dimensions shrink, outer pressures meet less resistance. As inner control becomes less, outer control becomes more necessary, if chaos and anarchy are to be avoided. Many welcome military training as a means of disciplining our youth . . . which, as it

early Christian movement and the Roman Empire. In his *Journal*, George Fox describes how a sustained practice of standing still in the light allowed him to see Christendom's spiritual captivity. It guided him to find allies in forging a movement of prophetic resistance and a renewal of integrative Christian faith and action. Writing *The Lamb's War* in prison, James Nayler articulated a program of far-reaching, nonviolent cultural revolution. We too may find our bearings with an apocalyptic perspective appropriate to these times. It may help us to renew the Quaker peace testimony to meet the challenges of the twenty-first century.

Some Historical Background

It is hard to know how far back to trace the origins of the present-day system. Certainly, militarism has enjoyed a hallowed status in the United States ever since the hot-heads at Lexington and Concord sparked a violent revolution that hijacked the robust argument and nonviolent resistance that American colonists were already waging against Britain's imperial domination.[59] But the present system began moving into its present configuration during the closing years of World War II, and a sketch of some lines of that development should begin there.

Well before the D-Day invasion of France, Allied forces were sketching political and economic blueprints for a postwar world order. Those arrangements culminated in August 1943 with the Bretton Woods Conference, which established the United Nations, the World Bank, the International Monetary Fund, and other postwar institutions. In view of those arrangements, the Rockefellers began explorations in New York that eventually led to the building of the World Trade Center in the late 1960s. A globally rational economy would be required to avert the kind of liquidity crisis that had precipitated the Great Depression. The United States, the massive military-industrial force that had proved since the fall of the Soviet Union twenty-five years ago. Some Friends even note that capitalism has achieved a global integration that allows the financial sector and its international capitalist class to feed parasitically on the economies of every nation. Capitalism has been perhaps the hardest factor for Friends to countenance. That is partly because it is such a complex, systemic phenomenon. It may also be partly because the Quaker movement arose when the capitalist system was at an early, promising stage. Friends were vibrant owners of small-scale, privately owned businesses and banks, before corporate giantism and global finance became dominant in the last half-century. And of course, most Friends are comfortably middle-class and we privately worry how significant changes in the economic system might affect our minor fortunes.

Finally, Friends are routinely scandalized by the juggernaut of right-wing Christianity and other neoconservative ideologies in American life. But few Quaker conversations on that subject rise above the level of "culture war" antipathies. Within our liberal frame of thought, we deplore the rigid belief systems of fundamentalists, the repressive sexual mores of conservatives, the stubborn refusal of the Right to grapple with urgent environmental concerns, the influence that the Religious Right exerts on the Republican Party, etc. These are valid concerns. But they rarely transcend the plane of bickering between different sectors of the middle class. Friends rarely consider the systemic role of right-wing religion and ideology today in relation to the other global forces just named.

The task before us is to find a perspective that unveils and demystifies the relationship between these phenomena today. That perspective is *apocalyptic*, as it was for John in first-century Asia Minor and for early Friends in seventeenth-century England. In the imagery of Revelation, John was taken up in the Spirit to heaven and guided by angels to see the true conflict between the

Part 3

Capitalism, Empire, and
the Military-Industrial Complex

Today, our expressions of the Quaker peace testimony often seem reactive, flat-footed. Many of us are stirred into action by particular outbreaks of military violence, the production of new weapons, the harsh tactics in the war on terror, etc. But these are episodic reactions to symptoms. Friends rarely countenance the larger systems that produce these symptoms. Our fitful reactions perhaps suggest that we are willing to live with the systemic inequities that, after all, serve middle-class Americans very well. We just hate to see the violence the system requires to enforce those inequities.

As suggested at the beginning of this essay, it is not enough to keep repeating that "war is not the answer." There is no good answer to a question that forces us into a false frame. We must *re-frame* the world in which we are living before adequate answers can be revealed to us. Having seen the ways early Friends applied the Book of Revelation to their own historical situation, we too may find that bizarre text helpful in framing the world-system of our own time and thus find our place of integrity and truth within it. Indeed, like the best modern science fiction, ancient apocalyptic texts can offer an "alienation effect" that helps us see our world more clearly. It may move us from a reactive, anti-war posture to a more robust practice of anti-war, the Lamb's War for our time.

Certainly, many Friends and others recognize that the United States is dominated by a "military-industrial complex." Some Friends also recognize that the United States has moved into an empire phase, more acutely

41

The early Quaker Lamb's War offers us a helpful bridge between the ancient world of Revelation and today's world. Certainly, a wide range of Reformation groups utilized the Apocalypse of John to interpret the tectonic changes afoot in Europe and Britain. Early Friends were the last of these groups and were able to interpret Revelation within the emerging possibilities of an early modern world. They re-read Revelation and other biblical texts in light of their deeply transformative experience, which helped them to re-imagine both religious and political life. In the decades to come, the Enlightenment's progress toward religious liberty and more democratic political processes set the template for modernity. In some respects, we can view the Lamb's War as one of the short-lived experiments that contributed to those eventual developments.

However, the early Quakers' vision was far more radical and utopian than that. The violent defeat and suppression of their initiative should not be glossed over too easily by a modernist triumphalism. The tragedians of ancient Greece wrestled dramatically with troubling paradoxes of human existence and Greek history that were later rationalized by the classical philosophers. Similarly, the early Quaker Lamb's War, in particular the suffering of Nayler, Fox, and many other early Friends, is a drama that should leave us with a lingering sense of tragedy, dissonance, and unease.[58] Now, more than 350 years later, we see the Enlightenment synthesis wearing thin, with neither religious nor political life rising to meet the challenges of a new age of empire. Can Revelation offer a useful framework for understanding the dilemmas of the Quaker peace testimony today? Can its post-ancient vision offer perspective on this postmodern era?

towards Men . . . however they be minded towards us: and by the Virtue of the Lamb . . . we are made to give our Goods to the Spoil, and our bodies to the Tortures of cruel Men, rather than defile our Consciences. . . . This hath God sealed in our Hearts, to seek the Good of all Men, Plot against none; but study peace and live quietly, and Exercise our Conscience faithfully toward whatever Government our God shall set up.[57]

Thus, Nayler shares the standard Quaker affirmation that civil government is ordained by God (see the other essay in this book). Although the aggressive rhetoric of his earlier political writings is gone, the logic of his Christian anarchism is still intact. Human laws have no bearing upon Friends, who live according to the law of Christ in their consciences. That life removes the occasion for any *just* human law to take hold of them. But if Friends are *unjustly* persecuted for their obedience to Christ's law, they will bear it and will refrain from plotting against any government. The revolutionary impetus is gone. Nayler expresses no expectation that Quaker witness will influence the new regime or the reactionary national mood that has welcomed it so jubilantly. He articulates a vision of a quiet people set apart.

James Nayler died after being attacked by unknown assailants on his way home to Yorkshire in October 1660. The quotation that begins this essay is among his last known statements.

It was four months after Nayler's death that Fox and Richard Hubberthorne drafted the emergency peace statement known to Friends as the "1660 Declaration." The other essay in this book treats that statement and the post-revolutionary shifts in the Quaker movement that slowly unfolded after the restoration of monarchy and the episcopal state church. But Nayler had already clearly articulated the future of the movement.

comprehensive political platform in early Quaker writings should not lead to the conclusion that early Friends were "apolitical."[56] Rather, the political logic of the Lamb's War must be reckoned according to its apocalyptic framing; it is *revealed* step by step.

Nayler offered a published apology to Friends for the way in which his actions had (temporarily) divided the movement and invited public wrath against them. But he never recanted to the government. In failing health, he was finally released from prison in September 1659.

Meanwhile, the English Commonwealth gradually collapsed after the death of Oliver Cromwell in September 1658. The son of Charles I was invited to return from Holland and was crowned Charles II in June 1660. He had made a statement in favor of religious toleration in May, and Friends were eager to greet the new monarch as a possible ally against the vindictive policies they expected to come from the new "Cavalier" Parliament. Several Quaker leaders published greetings. Nayler added his own statement the month of the coronation. It is worth excerpting here, as it interprets the preceding eight years of the Lamb's War and reframes the movement in the face of new and unpromising circumstances:

> O King! God hath in these Nations a People gathered by himself into his Light, who are known to himself better than to Men, and therefore have we suffered by Men under all the Powers that have risen in this Nation ever since God called us toward himself, by his Eternal Light and Spirit. And though we receive not our Laws from Man, yet we are not without Law as to our God, but have one Law-giver, even Christ Jesus our Lord . . . [and] from his Laws we may not depart. And by his Law in our Conscience, and the Power of his Spirit in our Hearts, we are ordered and guided to walk holily toward our God, and harmlessly

and his followers who are entered into the
Covenant which was in the beginning. . . . [The
Lamb has come] to take the Government to
himself that God alone may wholly rule in the
hearts of Men and man wholly live in the Work
of God.[54]

Nayler here asserts that the light of Christ in people's
consciences, particularly as it is brought into focus and
direct action by a gathered people, deconstructs and
reforms not only personal behavior but the entire
edifice of a culture.

Unlike Mao's Cultural Revolution of the 1960s, this was
not to be imposed coercively from above but stubbornly
waged nonviolently from below. Nayler admits that this
program requires a fierce faith:

Many are ashamed at the Lamb's appearance,
it is so low, and weak, and poor, and
contemptible, and many are afraid seeing so
great a power against him. Many be at work in
their imaginations, to compass a kingdom . . .
but few will deny all, to be led by the Lamb in a
way they know not, to bear his testimony and
mark against the world, and suffer for it with
him. . . . The Lamb's War you must know
before you can witness his kingdom. . . . He
that preaches the kingdom of Christ in words,
without victory, is the thief that goes before
Christ.[55]

People may imagine they know God's will and desire to
"compass a kingdom" by building a political platform
out of their ideas and their power to enact them. But to
trust Christ completely, to follow the Lamb wherever he
goes (Revelation 14:4), no matter the cost, as Nayler and
other Friends did, is an entirely different matter. This
amounts to an *anarchist* form of social revolution in
that Friends let it unfold according to the leadings of
Christ's Spirit among them, beyond their own
understandings and intentions. Hence, the absence of a

arraigned in December before Parliament in a sensational show-trial aimed to discredit both him and the Quaker movement generally. He was accused of blasphemously claiming to be Christ. At his interrogation upon arrest, Nayler interpreted the exalted language his followers had used in leading him through the streets of Bristol:

> I do abhor that any honors due God should be given to me as I am a creature, but it pleased the Lord to set me up as a sign of the coming of the righteous one. . . . I was commanded by the power of the Lord to suffer it to be done to the outward man as a sign, but I abhor any honor as a creature.[53]

Nevertheless, Parliament proceeded to stigmatize and savagely punish Nayler for blasphemy. But the real political horror of Nayler's act was exactly what he affirmed of its meaning: namely, *Christ risen and moving in the flesh of common people like himself.* Parliament could imprison Nayler, but it could not contain the collective incarnational reality of the movement itself.

Still, official persecution intensified and the show trial inspired mob violence against Friends, particularly around London. Nayler languished in prison, having been beaten, branded, and bored through the tongue, but steadfast in his witness. The next year, he published *The Lamb's War* from Bridewell prison in London (an expanded edition appeared in 1658). Here he articulated with breathtaking scope the movement's liberation struggle:

> Their war is not against Creatures, not with the flesh and blood but spiritual wickedness exalted in the hearts of Men and Women, against the whole Work and Device of the god of this World, Laws, Customs, Fashions, Inventions, this is all Enmity against the Lamb

without flattery, refusing to remove their hats before magistrates, prophesying by women, etc. Then he observes,

> and now you that call those small and frivolous things knows not the law of a pure conscience. For where the conscience is kept pure it counts nothing little that Christ commands or forbids . . . and here be your witnesses against yourselves, who calls that little for which you inflict such heavy punishments and long imprisonments and large fines; and for those little things, we are looked upon as not worthy to live in the nation, and in those things you call little do we appear to be transformed into the kingdom of Christ and out of the kingdoms of the world.[52]

Through such "frivolous" behaviors, Friends saw themselves obeying a sovereign authority alien to the consciousness of mainstream society. The Lamb's War enacted *infrastructural politics* that Friends believed would be more transformative than the superstructural politics of the new regime.

Nayler continued to operate in the north until the summer of 1655, when he was called upon to help with the work in London, which had begun the previous summer with spectacular success. His personal charisma brought the movement there to new heights. His writing became less politically engaged, however, and he was gradually drawn into an internal conflict among Friends in London, which is not the focus of our attention here.

But Nayler and a small group of followers carried out a symbolic action in Bristol in October 1656 that is significant to the Lamb's War. In an enactment of the triumphal entry into Jerusalem, Nayler played the role of Jesus, with his followers singing "Holy, Holy, Holy." They were arrested by local authorities, and Nayler was vanity, and the sons of men, who are become a lie?

. . . And you [in power] that have so much cried up the kingdom of Christ in words and yet have been bold to limit him in his kingdom (the consciences of his saints), therefore above all the rest you shall not escape unpunished. . . . Therefore now will I arise, saith the Lord . . . and I will appear for her [Zion] in the midst of her enemies, and I will gather the outcasts thereof, who have not been regarded, but have been scattered by you as the off-scouring of the world . . . for the world's outcasts are my jewels, and I will bring them to possess the gates of their enemies: even by the word of the Almighty shall this be accomplished; the day is near at hand.[50]

Nayler saw the tendency of events clearly. England's most radical Parliament dissolved itself the next month. Oliver Cromwell became the lord protector of the nation, calling and dismissing Parliaments and sometimes resorting to direct military rule over the next four years. Nayler wrote *To the Rulers of This Nation* in April 1654, in which he reminded the rulers that they had promised liberty of conscience during the Civil War. Men like himself had risked everything in fighting the king in order to have "liberty to profess Christ alone, to be king in conscience, and submitting alone to his pure law going forth of Zion, denying all laws that are contrary to that of Christ in the conscience."[51]

Since the war, as long as people like himself only *talked* of the kingdom of Christ, they were not persecuted. But now that Christ has gathered them to *enact* the kingdom through his rule in their consciences, they are persecuted. He goes on to list various Quaker behaviors and testimonies for which they are persecuted. These odd Quaker manners and everyday resistances were matters such as refusing to swear oaths, speaking

It was difficult for those in power not to infer violent threats from early Friends in such repeated warnings of "overturning." But Friends didn't seek state power, nor did they offer any new political model. Rather, they generated a nonviolent revolutionary spiritual ferment from below that civil power would have to accommodate as it spread or else lose control of the nation.

As Parliament continued to founder, unable to agree to abolish tithes, to establish definite religious freedom, or to stop the growing persecution of Friends, Nayler published *A Lamentation over the Ruins of this Oppressed Nation* (November 1653):

> O England! how is thy expectation failed, now after all thy travels? . . . Hast thou looked for reformation, but all in vain? For as power hath come into the hands of men, it hath been turned into violence, and the will of men is brought forth instead of equity. . . . Their houses are filled with oppression, their streets and markets abound with it; their courts, which should afford remedy against it, are wholly made up of iniquity and injustice, and the law of God is made altogether void, and truth is trodden under foot. And plainness is become odious to the proud, and deceit set on high: and the proud are counted happy, and the rich are exalted above the poor. . . .
>
> And this is not done by any open enemy; for then it had not been so strange unto thee; but it is done by those who pretend to be against oppression, and for whom, under that pretence, thou hast adventured all that is dear unto thee [i.e., in fighting the Civil War], to put power into their hands; and now thou criest to them for help, but findest none that can deliver thee. O foolish people! When will ye learn wisdom? When will ye cease from man, who is

... for Christ is risen, the true light shines, the glory of the Lord appears, and you are discovered to him.[48]

James Nayler and the Lamb's War

Early Friends understood Christ's teaching through human conscience to be not only the foundation for a restored Church but also to provide a new political basis. With Charles I beheaded and Parliament at odds both with the Army and with itself, there was an open moment for England's rightful sovereign, Christ within, to rule. In *The Power and Glory of the Lord Shining out of the North*, or the *Day of the Lord Dawning* (August 1653), Nayler denounced Parliament's stalemate and proclaimed good tidings from the north:

> and you that are in power, mind the promise of the Father, at the coming of Christ to his kingdom, "I will overturn, overturn, overturn, till it comes into his hand whose right it is [Ezekiel 21:27], and upon his shoulders shall the government be established" [Isaiah 9:6]. . . . And take notice how many have been overturned already, who have been limiting him by their wisdoms. . . . Oh that there were such a heart in you, to lay aside all your own wills and carnal consultations, and to take counsel at the Spirit of the Lord and be guided by his pure light shining into your conscience, which would bring you into the fear of the Lord and to depart from self-ends, interests and exaltations, and to follow the law of God in establishing laws for yourselves and others to walk by. . . . There shall be no rest until his kingdom be established above all mountains. Hear all ye powers of the earth, the Lord alone will reign.[49]

> There is a people come forth of the north that
> shall spoil Babylon.[46]

The Quaker anti-war began with confrontations with
local clergy in northern parish services, and spilled out
into the streets with preaching against immorality and
fine clothing and into the marketplace with
denunciations of unfair trading practices. It was not the
work of a few leaders but of large numbers of newly
convinced women and men seeking to discredit the
religious establishment and call in the streets for equity
and justice. This behavior soon had Friends arrested
and taken before local justices. Their unwillingness to
remove their hats, use deferential language, or swear
oaths soon landed them in prison.

There isn't space here to go into the wide-ranging ways
in which early Friends used words, symbolic actions,
and lifestyle behaviors to confront religious repression,
social hierarchies, conspicuous consumption, and
general immorality. It was a prefigurative politics of the
kingdom of heaven on earth, enacted within the idioms
of their English society. Today, Friends conceive these
behaviors as a set of timeless ethical values. But early
Friends framed their actions in urgent, militant terms as
the nonviolent revolutionary campaign of the Lamb's
War.[47] *Revolution*, an overturning, is not too strong a
word for the vision of the early movement. In his first
published tract, *To All That Would Know the Way to
the Kingdom* (1653), Fox announced,

> God is coming to judge the great whore, all
> manner of opinions, and all manner of sects
> and fellowships (as you call them) all manner
> of her forms, as every one that lives in God is
> coming to overturn and overthrow . . . he will
> overturn them, that he may establish his own
> truth . . . the terrible day of the Lord draws
> near, the beast shall be taken, and the false
> prophet, into the fire they must go. . . . Now
> shall Zion arise . . . and thresh the mountains

not escaped Babylon but were "yet in the suburbs thereof."[43]

The Lamb's War

In 1648, while still in the earliest stages of his ministry, Fox was sitting in a Friend's house when,

> I saw there was a great crack throughout the earth, and a great smoke to go as the crack went; and that after the crack there should be a great shaking. This was the earth in people's hearts, which was to be shaken before the Seed of God was raised up out of the earth. And it was so; for the Lord's power began to shake them, and great meetings we began to have.[44]

Fox interpreted the physical shaking that began breaking forth in Quaker worship in terms of the several earthquakes envisioned by John and some of the Hebrew prophets. This *experiential* reading of apocalyptic literature is central to the early Quaker sense of Christ's revelation as earth-shaking and transformative, both personally and socially. The inner conflict and transformation Nayler described above quickly moved out into social confrontation. Fox wrote:

> And the Quakers are risen up in the night of apostasy, and discover you all what you are in, and what you went from, and what hath been lost since the days of the apostles. And an earthquake is coming upon you that hath not been since the foundation of the world [Revelation 16:18], out of which earthquake we are come into that which cannot be shaken [Hebrews 12:27].[45]

> [N]ow the gospel of God is known, the power of God . . . on this the Lamb's day, whose sceptre of righteousness has gone forth, who will rule the nations . . . and make war in righteousness.

traditions, and cannot sit long in them, therefore turn one against the other."[39]

Fox understood the *False Prophet* to be preeminently the church's state-enfranchised, university-trained clerical ruling class who added ideological mystifications to the Beast's power. These are "the false prophets, which Christ said should come, and John saw were come, and how all the world wondered after them; how they filled the world with false doctrines, ways, worships, and religions."[40] This regime alienated people from knowing Christ within: "The eyes of people have been after men, and not after the Lord."[41] The way in which the clergy resorted to "the arm of flesh" in rallying magistrates and Parliament to repress early Friends only confirmed to Fox the demonic nature of the clerical establishment.

Babylon in early Quaker understanding represented impure faith generally, including but not limited to the state-sponsored church. Following John, Fox uses terms like "fornication" in the spiritual sense of adulterated religion. "This woman, the false church . . . is whored from the spirit of God, which is drunk with the blood of the martyrs and saints."[42] Moreover, *Babylon rides the Beast*; as the church provides religious legitimation for the state, so the state provides its church not only a near monopoly of religion but also lavishes it with the resources to build awe-inspiring buildings and other religious pomp (through a state-enforced system of tithes and other financial support).

Even the non-conforming churches benefit, so long as they do not fundamentally question the Constantinian establishment. Francis Howgill had been a preacher among Separatist groups that had withdrawn from the national church and formed independent congregations. But after his Quaker convincement, Howgill wrote that Separatists had not yet come to deny the *ground* of apostasy, only some of its *practices*. Thus, he concluded, even the most advanced among them had

Fox's central message that "Christ is come to teach his people himself and take them off the world's ways and religions" was a "second-coming" message. But simultaneously, it simply reasserted the reality that had been present and available during the entire 1,600 years of apostasy. Since the Reformation had come to a religious and political stalemate in England and on the Continent, early Friends believed that the Quaker breakthrough was the way forward, not just a new sectarian option. The Church was coming out of the wilderness in their rapidly expanding movement. The new Jerusalem was coming into view.

Friends understood themselves to be the faithful 144,000 (not understood as a literal number), a vanguard standing with the Lamb upon Mount Zion. There, Christ taught, gathered, and led them through his light in their consciences. This same Lamb was also the Word of God in Revelation 19, advancing a nonviolent conflict with the sword coming from his mouth, which was materialized through their words, both spoken and published, and their actions. Early Friends saw themselves as engaged in a struggle against the Beast, the False Prophet, and Babylon as they found them in the neo-Constantinian establishment of their day.

Fox understood the *Beast* to be preeminently the coercive power of the state-sponsored church, with its forced attendance and its clergy promulgating state ideology alongside Christian doctrine. The Beast that had taken control of the Church from the time of Constantine had persecuted the faithful ever since: "Christ in the flesh, the church fled into the wilderness."[38] Moreover, competing political aims and Scriptural interpretations within the imperial church had split it into warring and mutually persecuting churches, becoming the many heads of the Beast that John describes in Revelation 13. Thus, as Fox wrote, "the apostate Christians have sat since the apostles' days, in their rudiments, inventions, handiworks, and

Revelation. Fox writes in his *Journal* that in 1647, at the age of twenty-three,

> I had great openings concerning the things written in the Revelations; and when I spoke of them, the priests and professors would say that was a sealed-up book, and would have kept me out of it, but I told them Christ could open the seals, and that they were the nearest things to us, for the Epistles were written to the saints that lived in former ages, but the Revelations were written of things to come.[34]

Revelation is the only book of the Bible that receives an extended interpretation in Fox's writings.[35] Fox is our primary source for understanding how early Friends interpreted Revelation, in particular the four elements of the Dragon's power in the society of their day.[36]

The Beast, False Prophet, Babylon, and Babylon Riding the Beast

In line with the Spiritualist and Anabaptist reformers of the preceding century,[37] early Friends believed that the Church had gone into *apostasy*, had turned away from the Spirit and direct teaching of Christ, soon after the apostolic generation. Fox believed that John's criticisms of certain currents within the churches of Asia Minor in Revelation 2–3 indicated the onset of that apostasy. The gradual accumulation of traditions, outward sacramental rites, clerical and hierarchical establishments, extraneous beliefs, focus on Scripture as the primary authority—and most of all the Constantinian establishment of Christianity as the religion of Empire—moved the Church increasingly into alienation from the divine presence in each person's conscience. The true Church, a remnant present in all times and places, had gone into the wilderness (following the imagery of Revelation 12).

Years later, in *What the Possession of the Living Faith Is* (1659), Nayler described his convincement and conversion thus:

> I came to see the begotten of the father manifest in measure in me in the pure image of a holy child. . . . Christ formed in me as the scriptures witness. . . . I was made to endure the loss of all things, and to deny all things that ever this holy spirit did war against in me, which might in any way oppress this holy plant, or hinder its growth, owning his judgment in the light, upon whatever was in my heart or affections but him alone.[33]

The Lamb's War begins with this inner confrontation and the renunciation of anything that might "oppress" or "hinder" the life and progress of the Christ formed within. Harrowing though it was, this was generally the path of convincement/conversion among early Friends. Coming through inner conflict and personal transformation prepared them for the interpersonal, social, and political conflicts they would face in widening circles—with relatives and employers, in the marketplace, at the local parish church—often culminating with an appearance in court because of their preaching or behavior. Nayler's first imprisonment came within a year of his beginning to itinerate around the north of England.

Early Quaker preachers such as Nayler and Fox declared the coming of Christ through the light in each person's conscience. Those who were gathered by this apocalyptic message met in local groups to wait in silence upon Christ's direct teaching. Through deep inward struggle, they reached a sublime peace within and among themselves. But that very same peace moved them into prophetic confrontation with the state-sponsored Church. They interpreted their conflict with established religion by drawing on the Book of

Radicals like Salmon and Winstanley quickly discerned the hollowness of the military victory and the oppressive power of the new Puritan establishment. The war had simply placed power in the hands of a new ruling class with its own repressive and violent tendencies. Nevertheless, social space had been opened for something still pregnant with possibility. The more straightforward purposes of God were soon to be revealed in a purified people.

Whereas the essay on the other side of this book follows the early Quaker trajectory mainly through the writings of George Fox, this essay features the writings of both Fox and James Nayler. These two key leaders of the movement were eloquent writers about the Lamb's War. Nayler articulated more fully the political meaning of their struggle.[30]

James Nayler, a yeoman farmer from Yorkshire, spent more than eight years in the Parliamentary Army as a quartermaster. He occasionally preached among the ranks. He finally left the Army for health reasons sometime after the battle of Dunbar in September 1650, returning to his wife and three daughters on their farm.[31] Nayler was part of a small group of Army drop-outs and other radicals in his neighborhood. They had been in correspondence with George Fox while the latter was imprisoned at Derby 1650–51 (see the other essay in this book). Fox traveled to meet with them soon after his release, in late 1651. He quickly imbued these advanced spirits with a new sense of spiritual empowerment and purpose. At the same time, they added to his message a social and political impetus not evident in Fox's earlier preaching around the Midlands in the late 1640s.

After some weeks of hesitation, Nayler suddenly left home in early 1652, without bidding his wife or children farewell and not even thinking of any specific journey. He later remarked, "And ever since I have remained, not knowing today what I was to do tomorrow."[32]

present denouement of the war, he wrote to his former comrades in arms: "You have a commission from the Lord to scourge England's Oppressors. . . . The Lord here besmears himself with blood and vengeance, deforms his own beauty, hides his amiable presence under a hideous and wrathful form."[27] But in that very moment of vengeance, the sword of the Spirit will soon find them out: "Friends! Look about you, for the Lord is now coming forth [to] rip up your bowels, to search your hearts and to try your reins; yea, to let loose the imprisoned Light of himself in you." The light's revelation will overturn their present vainglory: "In an holy shame, you will reflect upon your present Employments. . . . the Lord hath shewed us . . . a more easie and sweet way of Victory; we can overcome by being conquered. . . . Oh, that sweet and meek Spirit of Christ!"[28]

That same month, Parliament declared England a commonwealth. Gerrard Winstanley took them at their word and founded a "Digger" commune for poor people in April, farming a tract of common land in Surrey. But as the experiment came under increasing legal and mob harassment, he reflected on the Civil War in terms similar to Salmon's:

> Victories that are got by the sword, are but victories of the Murtherer, and the joy of those victories is but the joy of Caine. . . . the Dragon hath fought against the Dragon, and one part conquered another . . . and the King of Righteousness hath been a looker on, and suffered them to break each other to pieces, that his power at last might come in. But now O England know this, that thy striving now is not only Dragon against Dragon . . . but thou now begin'st to fight against the Lamb, the Dove, the meek Spirit . . . and wilt not willingly suffer the Prince of Peace to have a house to dwell in upon the earth (which is humane bodies) but seekst to imprison, beat, kill.[29]

Part 2

Early Quaker Lamb's War

The Quaker movement began sixteen centuries after the start of the Christian movement, in very different historical circumstances. Early Friends, however, found a powerful template in the Book of Revelation for understanding the conflict that swirled around them and the persecution they suffered. They were by no means the first radical group in that period to draw upon Revelation. Many sensed the end of the world they knew when their king was beheaded. Monarchy was practically the only social order in human memory. But what new age was dawning?

The English Civil War had erupted in 1642 as the culmination of a long conflict between court and country; between royal prerogative and the more democratic impulses growing in Parliament; between the old, landed wealth of monarchy and aristocracy and the new, proto-capitalist power of the growing mercantile class; between the conservative royal policy of ecclesiastical governance and the restive, reforming forces of Puritan piety. By the time the war was finally resolved with the defeat of Charles I in 1648 and his execution at the beginning of 1649, the war had become for many a revolutionary struggle for the kingdom of God in England. Radicals, many of whom had fought on the side of Parliament, affirmed that God's hand was visible in Parliament's victory.

But at the very moment of military victory, some of the most radical visionaries saw that the nature and methods of the struggle were changing. In February 1649, within a month of Charles's execution, Joseph Salmon left the Parliamentary army. Reflecting on the outburst in Jerusalem began to overturn the confusion of languages and scattering of peoples at Babel. As described in mythic terms in Genesis 11, Babel (the primordial empire) was undone in its vainglorious project to build a tower to heaven. (Such towers in the ancient Near East were also defensive fortresses, so military might as well as god-like hubris are implied by Babel's tower.) The scattering of peoples, languages, and religions henceforth constituted the ancient world, down to John's time. The story of Babel (like the rest of Genesis 1–11) is more properly *anti-myth* than myth. That is, it repurposes mythic materials from around the ancient Near East, not to explain and justify the world as it is (as myth generally does), but to describe the human dilemma to be addressed in the Hebrew saga that begins in Genesis 12 with the story of Abraham and Sarah. Similarly, John uses a panoply of ancient mythic materials for the *anti-mythic* purpose of describing the end of the ancient world.

But rather than venture further into the labyrinth of Revelation, which has inspired myriad interpretations over the centuries, let us move on. We will now explore how early Friends re-read the Book of Revelation in the light of both their own powerful, pentecostal experience and the nonviolent revolutionary struggle it led them to wage, the Lamb's War.

Jerusalem. With the rapid expansion of the Christian movement, John's vision became reality. That is to say, pagan Rome, with its far-reaching military conquests and slave-based economic system, had succeeded so well in subjugating and integrating the ancient world (or the world as far as Rome knew it) that it reached the point of contradiction. Rome's success was its undoing. The political and economic coherence of the Empire demanded a spiritual and ideological coherence far greater than the thinly veiled farce of Caesar-worship.

From deep within the belly of the Beast had arisen a grassroots movement with a message of human liberation that undercut and delegitimized the Imperial cult of domination. The cross, the preeminent Roman instrument of torture and suppression of resistance, became the central symbol of the Christian movement's deconstruction of the Empire. It unveiled and mocked Rome's brutal power. As Walter Wink posits in Christian-Jungian terms, the resurrection of the Jewish Messiah, Jesus of Nazareth, is an objective fact of history; it spread rapidly and forcefully as a new archetype in ancient consciousness.[25] Or, in the work of Alain Badiou from a Marxist-atheist perspective, Paul's preaching of Christ established "the foundation of universalism." [26] That new universalism marked the end of the ancient world and its jumble of deities and patchwork of mythologies.

That turn of the ages, initiated at the cross of Jesus Christ, is implied in Luke's story of the Pentecost in Acts 2. Diaspora Jews and proselytes from all over the Empire were in Jerusalem for the feast. When the Holy Spirit, the new consciousness, took hold of the Palestinian apostles, they prophesied in languages the visitors recognized from their various adopted homelands. "What does this mean?" they asked one another in amazement.

The larger meanings of that moment took form over decades to come. But Luke hints that the prophetic she is described in purely architectural imagery as built of every kind of precious metal and mineral. But whereas Babylon is opulently *dressed* in appropriated commodities, Jerusalem is *herself* precious beyond all valuation. Finally, the marriage of new Jerusalem and the Lamb serves as the counterimage to Babylon riding the Beast. It is an eternal covenant in contrast to a quid pro quo power arrangement.

But John's portrayal of these divine counterpoints to the Dragon's imperial powers is entirely visionary and structural. It lacks the life-giving qualities of faith and community. That is the glaring weakness of the Book of Revelation. We have to look elsewhere for the internal dynamics of the movement, for example, in the passage of 1 Peter explored in this book's other essay. But Revelation's strength is that it offers the biggest of all "big pictures" of the conflict between two diametrically opposed forms of power.

Revelation as a Post-Ancient Text

We have examined only a small portion of the wide array of ancient mythologies and cosmologies that scholars have identified in the Book of Revelation. The text is a huge mural, a grand pastiche of ancient pagan and Hebrew worldviews. They are all brought to destruction, replaced by a new heaven and a new earth. A new Jerusalem, a new human community, descends to earth. So John envisions not the end of the physical cosmos but the passing of the ancient cosmologies that constructed "the world" in human understanding. This is implied by John's vision of the heavens rolled up like a scroll (6:14). The scroll refers to "the heavens" in human religious understanding rather than to the physical elements themselves.

In other words, *John envisions the end of the ancient, pagan, polytheistic world.* He had already experienced the end of his temple-centered Jewish world in are countered in Revelation by John's vision of four divine figures.

The Lamb, The Word of God, New Jerusalem, and the Marriage of the Lamb

Directly after the vision of the Beast and the False Prophet, John sees the Lamb standing on Mount Zion with 144,000 who "follow the Lamb wherever he goes. They have been redeemed from humankind as first fruits for God and the Lamb" (14:4). The Lamb is of course a symbol of Christ, the slaughtered Lamb who (as noted earlier) breaks the seven seals. As "first fruits," the 144,000 are not the full extent of the Lamb's redeeming work but the revolutionary vanguard in the conflict against the forces arrayed by the Dragon. Their symbolic number answers the unholy number of the Beast (666). It also matches the 12,000 saved from each of the twelve tribes of Israel (5:3–8) and resonates with the twelves mentioned in John's description of new Jerusalem, another symbol of collectivity (21:12; 22:2). The Lamb, the true lord of the cosmos, counters the Beast. The False Prophet is countered by another figure of Christ riding on a white horse. He is triply named "Faithful and True," "The Word of God," and "King of kings and Lord of lords" (19:11, 13, 16). Out of his mouth comes a sharp sword, suggesting that the mode of conflict is to be nonviolent—theological and spiritual rather than physical. Thus, he counters the ideological mystifications of the False Prophet.

Babylon is countered by the heavenly woman from chapter 12, who was driven into the wilderness but protected there by God for an appointed time. She represents both Israel and the Christian movement under persecution. She merges with the new Jerusalem, who appears to John "coming down out of heaven from God, prepared as a bride adorned for her husband" (21:2), who is later identified as the Lamb (v. 9). Symbolic of the community gathered around the Lamb,

The Beast and Babylon—political-military power and economic prosperity—form the first synergistic pair. The Caesars (and the Flavian emperors who had succeeded them by the time of Revelation) brought unprecedented territories, resources, and slave labor under Roman control and integration. Babylon thrived on the circulation of these material and human resources, expedited by Roman road building and the suppression of piracy on the seas. In turn, new wealth contributed to military might and imperial administration.

That synergy generates the third term, Babylon riding the Beast. This complex term is significant in its own right. Political-military power and economic life are two different forces. But their interaction is intoxicating, symbolized by Babylon's drunkenness while riding the Beast. She is drunk with power and with the blood of whoever gets in their way—and quite sure that "I shall never see grief." The vainglory of Babylon riding the Beast in turn generates the fourth term, the False Prophet, an imperial ideology that incorporates religious legitimations, mystifications, and "special effects." As the Empire prospered, great building projects added monumental splendor to Rome and many cities around the Empire. These expensive marble edifices awed the populace, making them ready to bear Caesar's coins and to offer a pinch of incense as a pledge of allegiance to the divine "lord of the cosmos." The great altar at Pergamum, for example, hallowed the Roman defeat of the Gauls, elaborated with pagan mythology.[24] Meanwhile, arenas in Rome and other imperial cities offered spellbinding spectacles of competition, combat, and slaughter. All these elaborations of political and economic power contributed symbolic force to the False Prophet's ideological justifications of Empire.

These four elements, continually reinforcing and furthering one another, account for the overwhelming success and dominance of the Roman Empire. But they even owned other slaves. Some slaves might live well, but not freely.

The export of material goods and slave labor from all over the Empire to cities, especially to Rome, was legendary even at the time. Moralists decried the conspicuous consumption of Rome's elites. In Revelation 18:4, a voice from heaven calls, "Come out of her, my people, so that you do not take part in her sins, and so that you do not share in her plagues." This echoes the words of Jeremiah 51:45 after the first destruction of Jerusalem. But whereas one might have left the first Babylon and gone somewhere else, the new Babylon is so vast that the call in Revelation is to dissociate with Babylon's economic regime, to side with its victims and join them. Again, this call is made most pointedly to the Nicolaitans and the followers of "Jezebel," who prefer to make compromises and live easier lives.

The Demonic Structure of the Roman Empire

We may now chart out the mutually reinforcing dynamics of the Roman Empire as envisioned in Revelation (see Figure 1). All four elements of this structure account for the overwhelming power and success of the Empire, but the diagonals are the most synergistic.

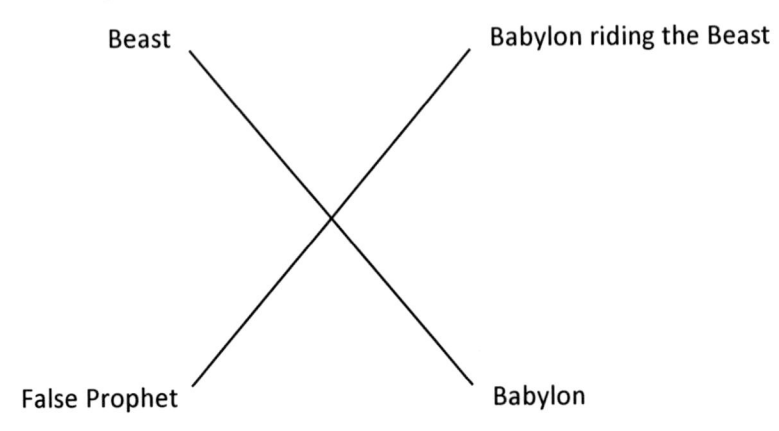

Figure 1: Dynamics of the Roman Empire

Moreover, *Babylon rides on the Beast*; that is, Rome's economic reach is premised on its political and military power—and they enable each other. Like economic power in any age, especially when combined with military might, Babylon is hard to resist. Even John admits, "When I saw her, I was greatly amazed. But the angel [who showed him the vision] said to me, "Why are you so amazed? I will tell you the mystery of the woman, and of the beast with seven heads and ten horns that carries her" (17:6–7). After demystifying some of the symbols for John, the angel flatly summarizes: "The woman you saw is the great city that rules over the kings of the earth" (17:18). Babylon arrogantly proclaims," I will never see grief" (18:8, echoing the original Babylon in Isaiah 47:7–8).

Chapter 18 envisions the destruction of Babylon. Kings, merchants, and shippers will weep and mourn for her. Indeed, the economic power of Rome rests respectively upon political force, trade, and circulation. Those who have been enriched by Babylon will share in her undoing. To emphasize the array of Babylon's economic power, Revelation 18:12–13 lists twenty-eight commodities imported to Rome. Last on the list is slaves (literally, "bodies"), an exclamation point to Rome's ruthless exploitation. Slavery was the determining economic basis of the Roman Empire. In Marxist terminology, it was the Roman "mode of production." Certainly, there were many free artisans, traders, merchants, peasant-farmers, etc., around the Empire. But slavery was the coherent core of economic life, just as the tradable commodity (including labor) is the basis of today's capitalist mode of production. Slavery took several different forms. State slaves, taken by military conquest, usually worked in mines, public works, galley ships, and other places of hard labor, seldom living long. Debt slavery placed one in bondage to a creditor. These slaves might be well-educated, skilled professionals who served as tutors to the children of the wealthy, handled large businesses, or making life difficult for those Jews and Christians who resist Caesar's blasphemous claims.

The third key demonic figure in Revelation is *Babylon*.[22] Whereas the Beast and False Prophet symbolize Rome's political-military power and the ideological mystification of that power, Babylon symbolizes the vast economic reach of Rome. As mentioned earlier, John names Rome "Babylon" because it is the second destroyer of Jerusalem. The feminine gendering of Babylon has been decried as misogynous by some modern feminist scholars. But Fiorenza[23] (herself a leading feminist biblical scholar) counters that Babylon is the demonic counterpart of the divine feminine figures of the heavenly woman in chapter 12 and the new Jerusalem in chapters 21–22. These figures complement the masculine demonic and divine counterparts of Beast, False Prophet, and Lamb. In any case, the feminine gendering of collective entities like cities is still commonplace today, usually without negative connotations.

"Babylon" may also represent the goddess Roma, worshiped by Romans and depicted on Roman coins. John describes Babylon in chapters 17–18. An angel gives him a vision of the "great whore," riding the Beast and adorned with gold, jewels, and purple and scarlet clothing. She makes the inhabitants of the earth drunk with the wine of her fornication. She herself is drunk with the blood of the prophets, Christian martyrs, and all who have been slaughtered (17:6; 18:24). Again, as with John's denunciation of Christians who compromise with Rome, "fornication" is about the seductions of religious and economic compromise. Prostitutes in ancient Rome sometimes wore headbands with the name "Roma" (see 17:5). Contractual sex with them had the connotations of sympathetic magic; it could inspire men to believe they were tapping into the good economic fortunes of Rome.

Revelation (it occurs in 1 John 4:3, but that John is generally associated with the Gospel of John). John of the Apocalypse ends his description of the Beast with a cryptic watchword: "If you are to be taken captive, into captivity you will go; if you kill with the sword, with the sword you must be killed" (v. 10). This may be a comment on the disastrous outcome of the Zealots' armed rebellion in Jerusalem. Violence against violence is already captive to the power that wields it. As we shall see, early Christian resistance to the Beast's captivity—the Lamb's anti-war—was a different mode of conflict.

John then sees a second beast rise, this one from the earth (13:11–18). It has horns like the Lamb but speaks like the Dragon. John names this beast the *False Prophet* (16:13). Perhaps John portrays these two beasts as the fulfillment of Jesus' prophecy (Mark 13:22) that false christs and false prophets will appear, performing signs and attempting to lead the disciples astray. Here the False Prophet performs signs and deceives the population, telling them to worship the image of the Beast. He even makes the image of the Beast speak. (Talking and even moving statues were a common "special effect" in cults of the ancient world, causing the gullible to marvel.[20]) The False Prophet also coerces all to receive the mark of the Beast "so that no one can buy or sell who does not have the mark" (13:17). Bearing the "mark of the Beast" may mean using Roman coins. Palestinian Zealots had renounced the use of Roman coins, which bore the image of Caesar. Jesus too had spoken ambiguously but in a similar vein when questioned about paying taxes (Mark 12:13–17).[21] Some Christians in Asia Minor may have begun to boycott commerce with Roman coins, which in most parts of the Empire would have entailed serious hardship.

In sum, the False Prophet represents the emerging ideological establishment of the imperial cult. Although the worship of Caesar was not yet enforced around the Empire, John sees the tendency of events and points to some form of economic sanctions that are already

The Beast, False Prophet, Babylon, and Babylon Riding the Beast

The Dragon stands on the seashore, and a *Beast* rises out of the sea before him. This Beast is described (13:1–10) in terms that echo the beasts described in Daniel (chapter 7), an apocalyptic book composed in 165 BCE that served as important resistance literature for Jews and then Christians living under empire. This Beast utters arrogant blasphemies and is given authority over all peoples, nations, and languages. His power is so overwhelming that they proclaim (or shrug?), "Who is like the Beast and who can fight against it?" (13:4). But those who follow the Lamb recognize the blasphemy of the Beast and will resist.

The Beast symbolizes the Roman emperor. His blasphemy is to exercise violent, oppressive power and proclaim himself divine, "lord of the cosmos." The number of the Beast, 666 (see 13:18), is probably intended as a numerical rendering of "Nero Caesar" in Hebrew letters. Nero's divine claims escalated the bizarre pretensions of the Caesars to new levels. He also initiated the first imperial sanction against Christians when he accused them of having started the great fire of Rome in 64. The Roman Senate and aristocracy hated Nero for his brutality and excesses; some even called him a beast. Nevertheless, he was beloved by many around the Empire. The Roman siege of Jerusalem was already well underway when Nero died in 69. So John would have assigned to Nero the fall of the city and the epic violence that ensued. The continuation of Nero's policies and blasphemous divine claims by succeeding emperors inspired John to make them all the same Beast.

Finally, mysteries around the death of Nero had led some to speculate that he hadn't really died. John alludes to this in 13:3, perhaps implying a demonic parody of the death and resurrection of Jesus. The Beast is thus the *antichrist*, though that term is not found in

Chapter 12, which forms the center of Revelation's chiastic/mirror structure, sets the book's conflict in terms that draw upon these ancient sources. A queen of heaven (symbolizing Israel/Mary/the Church) appears to John. She is about to give birth. Then John sees a great Dragon wreaking chaos in heaven and waiting to devour the child, who is destined to rule the nations as soon as he is born. But before the Dragon can devour him, the son is swept up to heaven and the throne of God. The woman flees to the wilderness, where God protects her for an appointed time. War breaks out in heaven and the Dragon is thrown down to the earth, where he begins to make war upon the rest of the woman's children (Jews and Christians). (Note the parallel in Luke 10:18, where Jesus sees Satan fall from heaven after the disciples have returned from their successful preaching mission.)

John's mythological re-presentation of the gospel story is his key to the conflict that pervades Revelation. As noted earlier, the cross and resurrection of Jesus have laid bare the violent machinations of demonic power.[19] Cast down from heaven (i.e., from the religious framework that has been used for millennia to justify violence), the Dragon now makes war on Israel and on all those who see through his power.

Having completed this brief introduction to Revelation, it remains now to view the key elements of Revelation's central conflict. The same elements also appear in early Quaker writings about the Lamb's War. These elements also shape this essay's exploration of the challenges we face today.

cataclysm of the seven trumpets and seven bowls may thus be understood as the release of the wrath "stored up" (see Romans 2:5) in the system, through the countless acts of individual hard-heartedness and institutionalized injustice that maintain it. Again, these are to be read less as historical events to come than as a mosaic array of the injustice and violence—the wrath— inherent in the structures of domination and *enacted all the time.*

The disasters of the seven seals, trumpets, and bowls are not willed by God or the Lamb but *allowed*: authority is *given* for these destructive forces (e.g., 6:8).[17] These desolations should inspire the inhabitants of the earth to repent and not participate in the forces that produce them. But hardness of heart and a merely episodic impression of events, rather than a visionary sense of the larger patterns, keep them from changing their ways (e.g., 9:20–21), just as the plagues of Egypt only hardened Pharaoh's heart. John's visions of destruction can sound harsh and vengeful to us today. Yet in our own time we face the cataclysmic consequences of countless selfish acts and institutionalized exploitation in the injustice, wars, and environmental crises all around us, all the time. John's visions point to the same reality in another age, using a different mythological language.

Collins places these many visions of destruction in a helpful perspective when she identifies ancient combat myths as an important framing of the Book of Revelation.[18] A variety of Semitic and Greco-Roman myths portray a struggle between two heavenly contestants for rule of the cosmos. One is a monster of chaos, often a dragon. Examples range from Babylon's battle between the god Marduk and the dragon Tiamat, Canaanite/Ugaritic texts describing a primal conflict between Baal and the sea, Egypt's Horus against Seth, and Greek mythology's combat of Apollo versus Python. The order and fertility of the cosmos typically hinge on the outcome of this primeval contest.

accede to its power, to the destruction inherent in that system, to the consequences of free human choices. The Lamb releases this onslaught of consequences as he breaks the seven seals on a scroll that symbolizes the destiny of the world. The Lamb (Christ) is worthy to do this precisely because by his death he has *ransomed* (5:9) out of slavery to the system those from every tribe, language, and nation who are willing to receive the freedom to serve the living God. Christ acts as God's redeeming agent on earth, freeing God's children from bondage.

Thus, Christ's death liberates people from slavery to *a system that is wrath itself.* His public execution at Roman hands allows the eyes of faith to see the travesty of dominating power. As Paul writes to the Christians at Corinth, "None of the rulers of this age understood this; for if they had, they would not have crucified the Lord of glory" (1 Corinthians 2:8). The crucifixion of Christ was a fatal mistake by the powers. Henceforth, violence and murder are delegitimized. The gospel reveals power of a different order, "so that your faith might rest not on human power but on the power of God" (2:5). Likewise, John witnesses that those who have seen human power unveiled, laid naked, can no longer accede to the power of the Beast.

After the Lamb breaks the seven seals, angels blow seven trumpets and pour out seven bowls of wrath. The place of angels in apocalyptic theology is important to note briefly here. In New Testament cosmology, angels represent a range of natural and social forces that Paul sometimes calls "powers." The powers are what Walter Wink calls the "interiority," or spirituality, of institutions.[16] (We all experience in one way or another the collective spirit of the various institutions in which we participate. Each affects us differently.) The powers are the good creation of God but are thrown into disorder and violence by Satan, the sower of deceit and disorder in creation. (See the discussion of civil power in the essay on the other side of this book.) The

Christian experience in apocalyptic terms,[14] but instead of using the visionary form of most apocalyptic literature, he writes letters to congregations. John similarly starts and ends Revelation as an epistle to seven churches in Asia Minor, but the middle of his letter explodes into exotic imageries and forms of apocalyptic literature. John's letter-bomb (as we might call it) makes it hard for us to notice the deeper connections with Paul's theology.

In Romans 1, Paul writes that "the wrath of God is revealed [apokalyptetai] from heaven against all ungodliness and wickedness of those who by their wickedness suppress the truth. For what can be known about God is plain to them, because God has shown it to them" (vv. 18–19). He explains that the invisible power of God can be intuited from the visible creation. But humans have exchanged the truth of God for a lie; they worship creatures (idols, human creations, images of earthly creatures) in place of the Creator. So what is the "wrath," the judgment? Three times Paul says "God gave them up" to the sinful behaviors that flowed from their idolatrous attachment to persons and things. He offers a laundry list of bad behaviors to make his point concrete (these include homosexual activity, but let's not get distracted by that here[15]). Paul adds that it is "God's decree that those who practice such things deserve to die" (v. 32). But God does nothing here. God simply *gives them up* to the soul-killing alienation and behaviors they have chosen. That is the "wrath"; God creates us as free beings, with all the wondrous and horrendous potentials that we continue to enact in history. (Jesus describes "the judgment" in similar terms in John 3:19–22: we enact it ourselves as we come to the light or flee from it.)

So the wrath that pervades Revelation—the great day of God's wrath (6:17; 16:4), the wine of wrath (14:10), the seven bowls of wrath (chapters 15–16), the winepress of wrath (19:15)—may be understood as God *giving up* Rome, along with the inhabitants of the earth who in 1 Peter (see the essay on the other side of this book), which focuses on local, social conflicts faced by congregations.

John acknowledges the widespread view that Rome's political power is too great to resist. He portrays "the whole earth" worshipping the Beast and saying, "Who is like the Beast, who can fight against it?" (13:4). He rejects the Zealot option of armed rebellion, which in any case brought nothing but ruin to Jerusalem. He instead seeks to foment an *anti-war* among the congregations of Asia Minor, a nonviolent apocalyptic conflict. It is to be waged by means of stubborn, open witness to the true lordship of God and God's Lamb, whose death on the cross has revealed Rome's idolatrous regime of sheer, brutal power. But the call to witness (*martyria* in Greek) is also a call to risk one's very life. In one vision, John sees the souls of the Christian martyrs hidden under the altar in heaven. They ask God how long before their blood will be avenged. John hears the answer that a certain number of martyrdoms must first be completed (6:9–11). But questions of how long and how many are linear and quantitative. In John's kaleidoscopic vision, the beginning, middle, and end are all present in constantly shifting patterns. To engage in the present struggle is simultaneously to partake of the ultimate victory of God and the Lamb.

Wrath

Similarly, the cycles of plagues and cataclysms upon the earth—seven seals, seven trumpets, seven bowls of wrath—are not necessarily predictions of historical events. They are patterned panoplies of *wrath*. Eruptions of divine wrath against human wickedness are part of the common stock of apocalyptic literature from which John draws.[13] But a passage from Paul's Letter to the Romans offers us insight into the early Christian logic of John's visions. Paul describes the was starting to face the same crisis that had nearly obliterated Palestinian Judaism.

John focuses the crisis most acutely upon the Caesars' blasphemous divine claims and the need for Christians to counter them openly. But in recent decades, scholars have come to doubt that the imperial cult of Caesar-worship was widely enforced in the 90s. Moreover, the active pursuit, interrogation, and execution of Christians, like that reported by Pliny the Younger to Emperor Trajan in the early second century,[10] was probably rare when John wrote. Still, some Christians may have experienced economic sanctions in the 90s, as I will note a little later.

In any case, John clearly seeks to intensify early Christian conflict with Rome. He is critical of congregations that are socially and economically comfortable with life in the Empire. He calls the Church at Laodicea "lukewarm" (3:15–16), complacent in wealth and ease. ("Lukewarm" may also play on that city's water system, which was fed by hot springs). John excoriates a certain female Christian prophet among the churches, calling her "Jezebel" (after the Philistine queen of Israel). She has endorsed "fornication" (probably meaning the mixing of Christian and pagan practices in accommodation to the surrounding culture) and the consumption of meat sacrificed in pagan temples (an issue also addressed in Paul's letters). John also attacks the "Nicolaitans," apostles who have brought a false teaching to the congregations. He doesn't describe their teaching, but the Nicolaitans may have been precursors to the later Gnostics, who generally advocated a quiet, esoteric mysticism that accommodated to the surrounding culture. Such teaching would have been anathema to John's insistence upon prophetic confrontation with Rome.[11] Thus, with John we hear a strikingly new voice at the end of the first-century Christian movement, far more oppositional to Rome than Paul's letters forty to fifty years earlier[12] and contrasting sharply with the counsel itinerated among them, at least in the years leading up to the writing of Revelation. Adela Yarbro Collins[9] persuasively suggests that John was originally Palestinian, one of many Jewish-Christian refugees from the cataclysmic fall of Jerusalem in the year 70. In response to a Zealot-led Jewish revolt in 66, the Romans destroyed the temple and all of Jerusalem, slaughtering untold thousands and dragging perhaps 70,000 off into slavery in various parts of the Empire. This was the greatest single catastrophe in Jewish history until the Holocaust of World War II. This John would have already experienced the end of his own Palestinian Jewish, temple-centered world. That would explain his portrayal of Rome as Babylon (the first empire to destroy Jerusalem, in 586 BCE). It would also account for the pervasive violence of his visions and his desire for vengeance against the Romans. Whatever the divine nature of his revelations, it is important to acknowledge John's post-traumatic condition and human frailty.

John's Palestinian origin is also suggested by his language. The Greek of Revelation is very awkward, as if John were thinking in Aramaic and Hebrew and then writing in Greek. Or perhaps a later scribe translated John's Aramaic/Hebrew text into Greek in a very literal, unidiomatic way.

Irenaeus, writing nearly a century later, believed that John's visions took place the year Emperor Domitian was assassinated (96). John mentions (1:9) that he was on Patmos, a small island off the coast of Asia Minor, at the time of his visions. He writes that he was there "on account of the word of God and the testimony of Jesus," which may simply mean that his itinerant prophetic ministry had taken him there. But Clement of Alexandria believed that John had been exiled there for his Christian witness, and that explanation has often been assumed by interpreters since. It might help account for John's urgent sense that the wider Church

> The whole structure of it breathes the art of God, comprising in the most finished compendium, things to come, many, various; near, intermediate, remote; the greatest, the least; terrible, comfortable; old, new; long, short; and these interwoven together, opposite, composite; relative to each other at a small, at a great distance; and therefore sometimes as it were disappearing, broken off, suspended, and afterwards unexpectedly and most seasonably appearing again.[6]

Some twentieth-century interpreters concluded that John was schizophrenic or took psychedelic substances. But Revelation's exotic imagery is more a matter of method than madness. The English poet and artist William Blake, who illustrated many of John's visions, bridges helpfully from Revelation to our modern assumptions about reality:

> "What," it will be Question'd, "When the Sun rises, do you not see a round disk of fire somewhat like a Guinea? O no, [responds Blake] no, I see an Innumerable company of the Heavenly host crying, "Holy, Holy, Holy is the Lord God Almighty." I question not my Corporeal or Vegetative Eye any more than I would Question a Window concerning a Sight. I look thro' it and not with it.[7]

Our task in this essay is to look *through* the phenomena of empire *with* the eye of faith.

Who was John? How did he come to such a way of viewing the world around him? Most interpreters conclude that this is not John the disciple of Jesus and/or the central figure in the writing of the Gospel of John. That Gospel has its own profound mysteries, but they are of a different kind.[8] Moreover, the name John was common in the first-century Jewish world. Since John of the Apocalypse addresses congregations in Asia Minor (modern-day Turkey), we may assume that he

Part 1

A Letter to Martyrs

The Book of Revelation, or the Apocalypse of John, was controversial even within the early Christian movement. It was the last book accepted into the New Testament canon. Probably written in the last decade of the first century, it has been used by various Christian groups over the centuries to speculate about the end of the world. Such approaches are termed "millenarian" (or "chiliastic"), in part because their predictions typically revolve around the obscure reference in Revelation 20:4 to a thousand-year rule of the saints.[3] But, as contemporary New Testament scholar Elisabeth Schüssler Fiorenza stresses, Revelation is not a timetable for predicting the end of history. Rather, it aimed to unveil (the basic meaning of the Greek verb *apokalypto*) the present situation of the early Christian movement in Asia Minor as it moved into growing conflict with the Roman Empire. The Book of Revelation is eschatological,[4] less in the sense of an end of history in the linear sense than as a vision of the demonic nature of an oppressive empire and God's victory over it.[5] The end appears in the structure of the book, not in its ending.

Fiorenza describes John's vision as *kaleidoscopic* rather than descriptive or narrative. Its panoply (impressive array) of visions and voices from heaven was probably bewildering even in its own day. It has fascinated, tantalized, or alienated readers ever since. The eighteenth-century commentator Johann Albrecht Bengel attempted to describe the effect of Revelation thus:

Introduction

today and the life-giving community that abides in the midst of it. So, although this approach may at first seem bizarre and irrelevant to peacemaking today, it may offer a more systemic vision of the challenges we face and the responses that are required. Friends have a great resource in the early Quaker witness as a bridge between the apocalyptic visions of John in the Book of Revelation and the apocalyptic destructiveness of today's regime. This systemic vision is an urgent need if we are to become more than reactive to the latest blights of the present system, if we are to become more than "anti-war."

early Quaker movement? And what does the anti-war look like in the twenty-first century? This essay explores these questions.

The essay on the other side of this book explores the Quaker peace testimony from its internal dynamics. It works outward toward social engagement but remains grounded in what it means to be a peculiar people finding its purpose in the world through the ways of peace. That essay begins with a meditation on the First Letter of Peter in the New Testament, then shifts to the early Quaker renewal of Peter's vision, and finishes with an exploration of how those dynamics might play out among Friends in the twenty-first century.

This essay bores into the issues from the other side, from the dynamics of a violent and exploitative world. It orients the dynamics of peace witness within that context. The sequence of sections in this essay mirrors the sequence in the other essay. It begins again with a New Testament text, this time the Book of Revelation, which was the primary source of Nayler's Lamb's War theology. It moves on to a further exploration of ways early Friends read the Book of Revelation in light of their liberation struggle in England of the 1650s. Finally, it contemplates the anti-war as a present-day phenomenon, structuring the issues again on the basis of Revelation.

This chiastic[2] structure of mirroring sequences is found in the Book of Revelation itself. Form gives clarity to content. The Book of Revelation overwhelms us with a flood of disturbing images and confusing symbols (rather like the flood of disturbing news that overwhelms us today). But when we identify the key structures of Revelation, we gain insight into its message for early Christians. Likewise, when we identify the structuring dynamics of our violent world today, a new clarity and resolve are possible. The key structural elements of Revelation constitute a lens that helps us recognize both the death-dealing structures of empire

Militant Peacemaking in the Manner of Friends

Introduction

There is more to the Quaker peace testimony than being "anti-war," reacting to each new outbreak of organized violence or the development of a new weapons system. Moreover, simply repeating that "war is not the answer" obliquely begs the question. The question is typically something like, "What should we do about Hitler?" (or Communist expansionism, Saddam Hussein, ISIS, etc.). This question forces us into a frame of thought alien to Quaker faith and practice at its best. We must instead stand fast in the same place James Nayler witnessed in 1659:

> There is a spirit that I feel that delights to do no evil, nor to revenge any wrong, but delights to endure all things, in hope to enjoy its own in the end; its hope is to out-live all wrath and contention, and to weary out all exaltation and cruelty, or whatsoever is of a nature contrary to itself.[1]

That testimony is a non sequitur to most talk about war and peace. Nayler, a former soldier, articulated the sublime peace we still find together in the stillness of Quaker worship. But he also wrote a tract entitled *The Lamb's War* in 1657 while in prison for his Christian witness. The tract describes an *anti-war*: an inversion of war; a nonviolent campaign against the entire social order that generates violence and war through the machinations of envy, greed, competition, and conflicts of interest. What was the basis for Nayler's theology of the anti-war? What did the Lamb's War look like in the

The Anti-War

Contents

This Side:

Militant Peacemaking in the Manner of Friends	1
Introduction	1
Part 1: A Letter to Martyrs	4
Part 2: Early Quaker Lamb's War	23
Part 3: Capitalism, Empire, and	
the Military-Industrial Complex	41
Part 4: The Anti-War	66
Conclusion: The One, the Alpha	
and the Omega, the X-Covenant	93
Endnotes	95

Other Side:

Introduction and Personal Testimony	1
Endnotes	15
Peace Finds the Purpose of a Peculiar People	17
Part 1: A Letter to "Aliens and Exiles"	20
Part 2: The Early Quaker Movement	41
Part 3: Peace Still Finds the Purpose	
of a Peculiar People Today	68
Endnotes	83
Works Cited for the Entire Book	88

The Anti-War

Other side

Peace Finds the Purpose of a Peculiar People

This side

Militant Peacemaking in the Manner of Friends

© 2016 Douglas Gwyn
All rights reserved. Except for brief quotations, no part
of this publication may be reproduced, stored in a
retrieval system, or transmitted, in any form or by any
means, electronic, mechanical, photocopy, recorded, or
otherwise, without prior written permission.

Editorial and book design: Charles Martin
Copyediting: Kathy McKay
Layout and design: Matt Kelsey

Published by Inner Light Books
San Francisco, California
www.innerlightbooks.com
editor@innerlightbooks.com

Library of Congress Control Number: 2016947701

ISBN 978-0-9970604-3-0 (hardcover)
ISBN 978-0-9970604-4-7 (paperback)
ISBN 978-0-9970604-5-4 (eBook)

The
Anti-War

Militant Peacemaking in the Manner of Friends

Douglas Gwyn

Inner Light Books
San Francisco, California
2016